This is
not a

FEMINISM

textbook

Copyright © 2023 Goldsmiths Press
First published in 2023 by Goldsmiths Press
Goldsmiths, University of London, New Cross
London SE14 6NW

A CIP record for this book is available from the British Library.

ISBN 978-1-913380-87-8 (pbk)
ISBN 978-1-913380-86-1 (ebk)

Director, Goldsmiths Press: Sarah Kember
Publishing Consultant: Susan Kelly
Editorial and Production Manager: Angela Thompson
Publishing and Marketing Assistant: Kobe Reynders
Cover design: Crxss Design
Design: Heather Ryerson
Copyediting: Adriana Cloud
Printed in the UK by Short Run Press Ltd
This book has been typeset in Neue Haas Grotesk Text Pro.

www.gold.ac.uk/goldsmiths-press

Goldsmiths
UNIVERSITY OF LONDON

This is not a

FEMINISM

textbook

EDITED BY

CATHERINE ROTTENBERG

Goldsmiths
Press

Contents

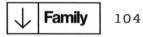

Introduction

CATHERINE ROTTENBERG

The late black feminist scholar bell hooks famously wrote that feminism is for everybody. This book was written precisely because feminism should, indeed, be for *everybody*.

→ **But, then, what exactly *is* feminism?**

Clearly if the answer to that question were straightforward, there would be no need for *This is Not a Feminism Textbook*!

Feminism, perhaps unsurprisingly, is a highly contested term. It has different histories in different countries and sometimes quite divergent definitions even within the same country. In the mainstream Anglo-American imagination, feminism is most often understood as the struggle for equal rights. But this is just *one* definition amongst many others, and in academic parlance, it is frequently considered the liberal definition. For radical feminists, feminism is not about gaining equal rights so much as ending – or as some might put it, smashing – the patriarchy and male dominance. And for Marxist and socialist feminists, the struggle revolves around the redistribution of material resources and wealth alongside efforts to democratise power.

Feminism not only has many histories and strands, but it also exists in different modes. Feminism is an identity or at the very least a way in which some people identify. Feminism is also a social commitment, a political project, a movement, a world view, an academic concept and a theoretical framework. Feminism

can even be considered a way of living one's life. These different modes of 'doing' feminism or of 'being' feminist clearly overlap and are at times indistinguishable from one another.

Despite their many differences, feminists do tend to agree on a few key issues. They concur that women across the globe have historically been and continue to be oppressed. But even such an ostensibly straightforward statement turns out to be not as straightforward as one might think, and raises a number of fundamental questions: How do we define women? Who gets included within this category? And who gets to decide who's included and who's excluded? Such questions continue to inform feminist debates, as readers will discover when reading the sections on Sex/Gender (p.10) and Trans (p.70).

The assertion about women's oppression also assumes that we already know what the nature of oppression is. But what exactly *does* oppression consist of and how do we identify its source and perpetrators? Is oppression primarily about legal discrimination or can it manifest itself in other ways as well? Is it about straightjacketing women in and through normative

expectations, such as the expectation that women become mothers and caretakers, or that they emulate femininity and so-called feminine traits? Is oppression restricted to forms of physical violence or does it also include psychic violence? Can we understand oppression as necessarily including all of these dimensions, and, if yes, who then should be held accountable for women's oppression?

Whilst the oppression of women may appear foundational to feminism, certain strands of feminism think the term is too broad and/or imprecise. Consequently, some feminists restrict their discussion to women's discrimination, whilst others highlight patriarchal domination. Ultimately, how we understand, describe and analyse women's oppression has to do with how we conceive human nature – namely, what makes humans *human* – as well as how we understand the way in which hierarchy and power relations are created, maintained and reproduced within our societies.

All of these perceptions are also inextricably linked to how we envision a more just society and what we consider to be at the very heart of the struggle for social justice. So even though feminists tend to agree that women's oppression – however it is conceived – must end, this seemingly straightforward statement is also misleading, since feminists often have diverging ideas about how to uproot women's oppression. The solutions range from legal reform to total revolution.

And, indeed, even a cursory look at feminist movements in the twenty-first century – from #MeToo, which highlights sexual assault and harassment, through the Global Women's Strike, which focuses on the gendered division of labour within capitalist societies, to the South American Ni Una Menos (Not One Less) movement, which mobilises against gender-based violence – reveals the varying ways in which feminists have envisioned the end to women's oppression and how they have fought to achieve their goals.

In short, there is nothing simple or straightforward about feminism.

Whilst complexity can and has been seen as a political or theoretical weakness, this book presents the opposite view. As readers will quickly discover, feminism exists as a dynamic concept, political horizon and movement. Feminism comes to life in debate, in political action and quite often in theoretical and political disagreement. It comes to life when its boundaries are challenged and its key ideas are tested, since it is precisely the engagement with new ideas, self-reflexive critique and the beliefs of new generations of activists and thinkers that help transform our notion and praxis of feminism. Feminism derives its power and enduring influence precisely from this dynamism.

This is Not a Feminism Textbook does not attempt to flatten out feminism's complexities. It does not attempt to define feminism once and for all or to offer a comprehensive guide to the history of feminism. Nor does it attempt to provide a comprehensive overview of the contemporary state of feminism.

Rather, this book aims to introduce readers to some of the current debates, terms and issues within contemporary feminism. The entries are written by feminist academics in the Global North, many of whom have themselves been actively involved in these debates, both within their scholarship and in their political activism. The contributors' perspectives will inevitably be shaped by their positions. Yet, we do not believe that these limitations will impede the book's overarching goal, which is to spark readers' interest, curiosity and desire to know *more* about feminism.

Sex/Gender

CELIA ROBERTS

What do we mean when we say 'sex'? And is there a difference between sex and gender?

Sex in Biology Textbooks

✛ **Genetic sex** refers to the 'sex chromosomes', X and Y. Having two copies of the X chromosome means a person is genetically female. Having an X and a Y means they are genetically male. There are many people with other combinations.

✛ **Gonadal sex** refers to the absence or presence of ovaries, testicles, and certain genital structures.

✛ **Anatomic or phenotypic sex** describes the so-called secondary sexual characteristics that generally develop at puberty, including facial hair, body shape, and breasts.

→ | ## Sex

The word 'sex' is generally used to describe sexual practices. Interestingly, in English, sex as a sexual practice is something we have, not something we do (i.e., we 'have sex'). In other languages, and also in English slang, sex can also refer to genitals. This connects to another scientific meaning of sex that is fast becoming redundant: the notion that sex refers to kinds of bodies (something that we are, not something we do). In many sports, for example, athletes compete in male or female events based on their body type.

In biology textbooks, a person's sex is expressed by their bodies at three, typically connected, levels: the genetic, the gonadal and the anatomic or phenotypic (see: Sex in Biology Textbooks, left). Sex, in this way of thinking, is the result of the sequential unfolding of genes and the development of genitals, reproductive organs and bodies from conception through birth, puberty and ageing to death. Sex hormones play a huge role in these unfoldings, shaping genitals and bodies (and, interestingly, sexual desire, which takes us back to the sex we 'have').

In European science and medicine, since the mid-eighteenth century at least, this understanding of sex has grouped people into two categories (male and female), thus also producing a diversity of pathologised others who do not fit neatly into these boxes. This framing, commonly referred to as 'the sex binary,' emphasises particular biological differences and similarities between and within groups, ignoring the many ways in which people placed in

opposing categories are alike and the complex differences among those in either category.

Broader concepts of reproduction, evolution and what it means to be human shape this understanding of sex. Probably because of the connections between the sex we have and the sex we are (or are supposed to be!) on the one hand and the possibility of reproduction on the other, humans have intensely focussed on genitals, bodies and sexual desire when studying and describing sexual differences. Like many sexually reproductive creatures, humans make babies through bringing together sex cells (eggs and sperm) that have half the genetic content of these bodily cells to form a new being with a full complement of genes. Although with the help of medical science this kind of conception can now be done outside the body, it is most commonly achieved through reproductive heterosexual sex.

Historically, the concept of sex has been used to control and oppress people (and some animals). Sex has been framed not only as a male-female binary (pathologising those who are not clearly of one physical sex) but also as a hierarchy in which maleness is privileged. In Euro-American and many other cultures, as feminist scholars have shown, female genes, genitals and bodies have long been described as inadequate, weak, lacking. Women (both

John Money and Anke Ehrhardt

Money and Ehrhardt were psychologists who worked together at the Johns Hopkins Gender Identity Clinic in the 1960s. (This clinic was one of the first in the world to offer 'sexual reassignment surgeries'.) In 1972, they published *Man & Woman, Boy & Girl: Gender Identity from Conception to Maturity*, which developed the concept of gender as a set of socially produced roles. Money is today regarded as a highly controversial figure, in part because of his long experimental engagement with twins Brian and David Reimer, both of whom committed suicide as adults.

A Feminist Sociologist's View of Gender

In 1972, reviewing the psychological and psychiatric literatures, British sociologist Ann Oakley wrote, 'The consensus of opinion seems to be that … [biology's] role is a minimal one, in that the biological predisposition to a male or female gender identity (if such a condition exists) may be decisively and ineradicably overridden by cultural learning' (Oakley, Ann. *Sex, Gender and Society*. Temple Smith, 1972, 170).

those whose genes, genitals and bodies are designated female and people who live as women without all or some of these characteristics) have been told their sex renders them incapable: of intellectual or physical labour, of rational thought, of certain spiritual or cultural practices. Feminists across the world have railed against such assertions, arguing and acting strongly against them both individually and collectively.

Importantly, biological science has clearly demonstrated that the sex binary is an imposition. In fact, human sex is complex and various and it changes over any person's life. Some people strongly desire to change their genitals and bodies; others enjoy or accept what they have. Some people's genes or genitals or reproductive bodies are atypical, and many of us do not desire reproductive heterosex! Here's where the concept of gender comes in.

→ Gender

Gender, a word that has very successfully made its way from academic texts to common parlance in less than 50 years, was repurposed from its original use in linguistics to describe the social complexities of sex – that is, to denote the multiple and fluid ways in which sexual differences are lived by humans as social animals. Interestingly, we still do not tend to speak of the gender of animals. They still have only sex, whereas we humans increasingly have only gender. (See: Feminist Biology p.18). Initially used in 1960s' psychiatric discussions of 'transsexual' people (to use the American terminology of the times), the term referred to clients' sense of self, which did not align with their natal genes, genitals, or bodies (see: Trans p.70). In highly controversial research on the connections between genes, genitals, bodies and lives, now-infamous researchers John Money and Anke Ehrhardt also used the term to argue for the radical separability of these phenomena (see textbox: John Money and Anke Ehrhardt). Feminist scholars, including British sociologist Ann Oakley, saw the political potential in this idea and retooled gender as a way to highlight the oppressive forms of socialisation shaping the lives of those designated as female. Thus the sex/gender distinction was born: a distinction in which sex refers to biological differences and gender to social ones (see textbox: A Feminist Sociologist's View of Gender).

Continually revised and recast across the last four decades, the sex/gender distinction has arguably now reached breaking point. Gender has taken centre stage and is increasingly seen as determining what we understand as sex. Indeed, American feminist philosopher Judith Butler famously argued in the early 1990s that sex was the outcome of repeated gendering acts; she did, however, exclude genes and hormones from such claims. (See: Judith Butler and Performativity p.16). In both queer and mainstream cultures today, sex is figured as malleable and as a zone of experimentation, even play. In *Testojunkie*, Paul Preciado, for example, writes lyrically of his use of testosterone to reshape his sex (his body, his desires and the sex he has). Rather than a binary, sex and gender are arguably becoming more and more like each other. We now need new models of how to think of the relations between genes, genitals, bodies and lives (see: Sex/Gender p.10 and Feminist Biology p.18).

Binary

The term 'binary' comes from logic and is widely used to refer to a pair of concepts in which the meaning of one is merely the absence of the other, such as off/on. This can be described as an 'A - NOT A' binary.

In European thought there are many binaries, including nature/culture, White/non-White and Man/Woman. The latter is the so-called sex (or gender!) binary. It implies that women are defined by not being men, or that femininity is the absence of masculinity.

Many feminist scholars have argued that binary thinking is hierarchical and inaccurate and has multiple deleterious effects on human and non-human life. This is particularly true of the sex and gender binaries which conventionally both figure maleness or masculinity as the valued norm and femaleness or femininity as a devalued absence or lack, and pathologise any forms of sex or gender that are not contained by these two 'opposing' or 'complementary' figurations.

NORBU GYACHUNG/UNSPLASH

In Euro-American cultures, sex/gender profoundly shape childhood experience.

From well before birth, the sex of a baby is typically revealed by ultrasound and often shared with family and friends. So-called gender reveal parties are increasingly common (note that these are not called 'sex reveal' parties), although they are also starting to be criticised. At birth, a baby's physical sex is decided and recorded, and often marked socially through clothing, toys and greeting cards. Psychological research shows that parents and other adults unconsciously engage with babies differently according to their revealed sex: boy babies are spoken to with more excitement and physically moved more; adults tend to hold them facing outwards more often than they do girls. Girl babies are talked to and handled more gently. As children grow, these differences become more marked. Boys are encouraged to run and climb, to hide their distress and to play with toys that represent objects such as cars and trains, or that involve building. Girls are encouraged to become aware of themselves and others through playing with dolls and animal toys, experimenting with clothes and engaging in role play centred on nurturing. These differences are highly elaborated in consumer cultures: think of pink and blue sections in toy stores. In recent decades, feminist activists have worked hard to dismantle these kinds of formations, exhorting toy manufacturers and shops to break away from allocating toys to specific sex/genders, encouraging preschool teachers and parents to be more aware of their actions and language and encouraging clothing manufacturers to produce more gender-neutral items.

These kinds of critical discussions often evoke the idea of gender stereotypes, arguing that children should be freed from dominant gender norms and expectations and pushing against ideas that gendered behaviours are in any way natural (that is, the outcome of sexed bodies or brains). Critics tend to assume that adults' conscious or intentional actions can break down deep-seated behavioural and linguistic norms, under-emphasising the importance of children's relations with each other. Feminist research has shown that even preschool-age children police each other in relation to sex/gender.

In contrast to feminist activists, psychologists and behavioural scientists understand particular kinds of behaviours (forms of play, preference for certain toys) as measurable and reliable indicators of something intrinsic to children that speaks to their sex. In research on girls with Turner Syndrome, for example, participants' interest in rough-and-tumble play is linked to their genetic difference to other girls (people with this syndrome have just one copy of an X chromosome). Clinical investigations of children who identify as gender-diverse or trans also explore play and toy interests, as well as choice of clothing and modes of movement and many other factors. These kinds of investigations assume that play and toy preferences can be expressions of an intrinsic gendered self.

We run up against several difficult questions here:

◘ What meaning or value should we ascribe to cultural norms of sex/gender? Is there anything positive in sex/gender differences?

◘ Is gender neutrality a good thing to aim for? Or should we be looking for the end of gender itself?

◘ How should we respond to children's desire for gender (both their own and others')?

◘ How can we open up children's lives to as many options as possible without producing negative connotations around certain behaviours or norms?

◘ Thinking more practically, if a particular child is attached to toy trucks, rough play and wearing blue, for example, should we try to divert them from those attachments? Would or should we feel differently about that child if they have male or female genitals? Or XX, XY or a single X chromosome?

◘ Are adults projecting cultural values back into children's worlds? Is it easier to think about the relative simplicity of children's worlds than to think about adults and social norms?

→ Judith Butler and Performativity

Butler's work has had a huge impact on how academics and activists, and arguably the wider public, understand sex/gender.

North American feminist philosopher Judith Butler has been publishing books since the early 1990s. In 1990, their book *Gender Trouble* – a complex philosophical text – argued that gender is performative of sex. This is a very specific claim, based on a theory that, in some instances, language produces reality – the key example is the marriage vow (saying 'I do' means you are married). Butler argues that the myriad ways we talk about and do gender (the ways we use pronouns, the clothing we wear, the way we move our bodies, for example) produce and thus 'perform' sex. For Butler, sex is not 'natural', and gender does not arise from sex. Instead, sex is the outcome of endlessly repeated gender(ing) acts. In Euro-American cultures, we tend to think of sex (and the sex binary) as biological and thus 'natural'. Butler argued that this is a cultural phenomenon, and that if we could do gender differently – if we could resist and reshape gendering practices – our understandings and experiences of sex would also change. Some physical differences (e.g. genes, hormones, genitals) would remain but could be understood and valued very differently. Arguably, this is happening today in some places. The pushback against gender reveal parties and changes to pronoun use are two examples.

A core strand of Butler's argument about sex/gender stresses the symbolic and material violence associated with the policing of sex/gender norms.

In the 1990s, Butler's argument was well received but also widely misunderstood to mean that somehow gender (and therefore sex) was a matter of choice or conscious action. Readers understandably took the term performativity to imply something that people could decide to do: a deliberate performance, like a show. In subsequent philosophical books, *Bodies That Matter* (1993) and *Excitable Speech* (1997), and a more accessible volume, *Undoing Gender* (2004), Butler has strenuously argued against this idea. Their use of 'performative' does not imply control or choice (although resisting norms is something Butler values!). Butler's interest in psychoanalytic theories of the development of a self is significant here. According to psychoanalytic perspectives, there are many ways in which we become people that are beyond our conscious control. We cannot will our gender to be a certain way because we are social and desiring beings,

immersed in specific cultures. Importantly for feminist and queer politics, this does not mean that change is impossible! If gender (and thus sex) is performed in literally millions of daily acts, then it can be done differently. Such change is necessarily cultural and collective – it has to be done by many people and in many times and places to have strong and lasting effects.

A core strand of Butler's argument about sex/gender stresses the symbolic and material violence associated with the policing of sex/gender norms. Those who challenge sex/gender conventions – physically or linguistically, through movement, appearance, use of language, expressions of sexual desire – are frequently subject to violent acts. In recent years Butler has highlighted the violence of anti-trans activists who refuse to engage with feminist and queer scholarship on the complexities of sex/gender, instead insisting on reductive understandings of biological sex. In both the US and UK, public debate on the significance of bodies, behaviours and desires are increasingly heated as long-term sex/gender regimes based on binary modes of thought are challenged.

→ # Feminist Biology

Feminist scientists understand the multiple ways in which sexist ideas pervade science.

Sexism is active in the formation of research questions, the funding of research, the practices of experimentation and data collection and the analysis and publication of findings. Sometimes these forms of sexism are obvious (when men are used to represent humans in an experimental setting, for instance) and sometimes they are subtle (the words used to describe body parts and bodily functions, for example: Why, as feminist biologist Sari van Anders asks, is semen not called 'penile mucus', when vaginal fluid, which is often called 'mucus', is not actually mucoid?).

For many decades now, feminist scientists have systematically exposed these forms of sexism. They have also undertaken new, anti-sexist, experimental work. American biologist Anne Fausto-Sterling, for example, has studied the development of sex/gender in human infants and children. In a series of studies inspired by Dynamic Systems Theory (which understands development as the outcome of multiple, complex processes), Fausto-Sterling and colleagues have explored the interactions of culture and biological development, including visual systems, movement capacities, cognitive development and sensations. Tracking the onset of sex/gender from conception through birth and early childhood, they show how adults unintentionally and intentionally produce sex/gender through the interactions of daily life: the way they speak to babies, the clothes they dress their children in, their practices of physical care. Importantly, this emphasis on social practices does not mean that Fausto-Sterling's team argues that sex/gender is not physical. Indeed, their research shows that social experiences have physiological effects. In her more theoretical work, Fausto-Sterling argues that sex/gender differences are best described as falling along a wide continuum. Rejecting binary thinking when it comes to either biology or culture, she insists that life is far richer and more complex than such thinking allows.

>KEY ELEMENTS *of all* REGIONS<

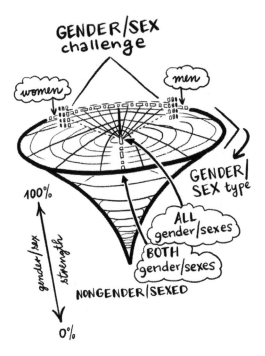

GENDER/SEX
challenge

women   men

GENDER/
SEX type

100%

gender/sex strength

ALL
gender/sexes

BOTH
gender/sexes

NONGENDER/SEXED

0%

Queer biologist Sari van Anders similarly designs research projects to challenge reductive ideas about sex/gender. With her research team at Queens University in Canada, Van Anders has explored the complex physiology and sociality of both human and non-human animals. Over two decades, these projects have led her to propose a new theory of gender/sex called Sexual Configurations Theory. Importantly, this theory explores sex in both its basic meanings: that is, both gender/sex and the sex we 'have' (i.e. sexual practices). Rejecting binary thinking, Sexual Configurations Theory relies heavily on concepts of range, diversity and strength. Any individual's identity at a particular point in time is understood as the expression of a pattern of configuration: how important sex/gender is to them, how singular or diverse their attraction to kinds of others is; how attached or resistant they are to cultural norms. This theory is designed to move beyond scientific papers into cultural life. Diagrams such as the one above (Fig. 1) are meant to help individuals think deeply about their own sex/gender and sexual proclivities.

Fig. 1 Sari Van Anders' Sexual Configurations Theory, originally published in *Mapping Your Sexuality: From sexual orientation to sexual configurations theory,* a zine written by Alex Iantaffi and Meg-John Barker, with ideas from Sari Van Anders and illustrations by Julia Scheele. Reproduced with permission from Julia Scheele.

Sexuality

CELIA ROBERTS

Sexuality is both deeply personal and profoundly shared.

→ Sexuality is Social and Political

Sexuality – both our sense of our own desire and the practices we engage in – occupies a highly ambivalent position in Euro-American cultures. Widely understood as natural, necessary and ubiquitous, sexuality is also often controlled, regulated and condemned. In many ways, sexuality is highly involved with power: religion, schools, governments and families all try to shape our sexual desires and practices along particular lines. From early childhood, we are told in one or way or another that there are appropriate and inappropriate forms of sexual expression, and that adults are monitoring what we do. Many forms of sexual practice are illegal and/or socially condemned, whilst others are fostered and celebrated. What is seen as unacceptable or worrying varies significantly across time and place, and differs across particular families and other social institutions, but everywhere limits are imposed.

Despite this, many of us experience sexuality – at its best, at least – as an expression of emotional and physical freedom. Sexuality seems somehow to be outside society, a liveliness arising from within that speaks to something profound about who we are. As a kind of energising force, sexuality brings us in touch with our physical bodies and our unconscious minds – it can catch us unawares, sculpt our dreams and shape the course of our lives.

From the late nineteenth century to the present moment, sexuality has been shaped by the development of sexual science, which attempted to take it out of the historical grip of morality and religion and place it under the cold light of rational investigation. Various forms of experimental and clinical practice, such as psychoanalysis and sexology, fostered the notion that our sexuality is core to our identities and that sexual truths can and should be pursued and spoken. With much – but never complete – success, scientific accounts tried to pin sexuality down, to name and (when needed) develop the technologies and practices to tame it.

Political campaigns and cultural representations of sexuality (in films, novels, songs and in online media) respond to, and in turn inspire, moral and scientific elaborations of sexuality. Anal sex between men, for example, was banned in England for many centuries. In the 1950s and '60s, however, activists successfully challenged British laws to decriminalise homosexual acts between consenting men over the age of twenty-one, in part based on scientific recognition that homosexual desire was not a disease. This did not mean the end of discrimination, however. In the late 1980s, the Thatcher government passed legislation prohibiting the so-called promotion of homosexuality in schools, banning discussion in sexuality education classes and forcing the closure of many lesbian and gay student organisations and groups. Again, activists worked to get this legislation repealed in the early 2000s, in part through aligning with scientific arguments that homosexuality cannot be promoted because it is biologically determined.

The HIV/AIDS Epidemic

The HIV/AIDS epidemic, which started in the early 1980s, permanently transformed sexuality research and sexual politics. The then-deadly nature of AIDS and the rapidity of its spread through particular populations invigorated intense activism and forced many governments to turn their attention to the complexities of sexualities and to listen to the work of social scientists and feminist scholars. In a time of great fear, sexuality researchers articulated important new findings about the multi-faceted relations between sexual identities, desires and practices. Research into homosexual sex, for example, found that campaigns advocating safer sex needed to address heterosexual men who also had sex with men. Research into the epidemic also highlighted the huge importance of community attachment, that is, people's identification with others like them, to their willingness to embrace changing sexual norms, like using condoms. Feminist research also detailed the ways in which heterosex was shaped by long histories of gender inequalities and cultural understandings of the biological underpinnings of men's and women's sexual desires.

Feminism has always been interested in sexuality, which is not surprising given the connections between sexuality and reproduction and sexuality's entanglements with power.

The last two centuries of feminist politics replicate wider cultural ambivalence about sexuality: feminists have tried to protect women from male sexual aggression and also tried to open up space for women (and others) to freely express their sexual desires. At various points in time, this inherited ambivalence has caused enormous rifts among feminist groups; in 1980s US politics, for example, it led to the so-called Sex Wars (see opposite, The 1980s North American Sex Wars).

In the midst of the Sex Wars, American anthropologist Gayle Rubin bravely attempted to diagram the dominant forms of cultural ambivalence about sexual practices (see Fig. 2). At the centre of her drawing were heterosexual, long-term partnered activities undertaken in private with people of similar ages. She describes these as the charmed circle: such behaviours were understood culturally, scientifically and religiously as acceptable and natural, not to be controlled. On the edges of the circle, cast out into critical scrutiny and even condemnation and legal and medical control, were sado-masochistic and homosexual activities, sex in groups and in public places and intergenerational and paid-for sex. Some of these activities were a source of serious friction between feminists. Rubin's diagram has been widely used and republished and captures some important enduring elements of feminist and cultural debates around sexuality. It is also very much of its time and place – it does not deal with sex occurring between people of different ethnicities or religions, for example, which may be much more important in other contexts. The HIV/AIDS epidemic, which began during the Sex Wars, had a huge impact on how these issues were discussed going forward (see The HIV/AIDS Epidemic, p.21).

We are often tempted to think about sexuality through the lens of progress, that is, to feel that things have gotten better or that we are freer than we used to be. Whilst some important legal and cultural changes have occurred in some places – for example, the decriminalisation of homosexuality, the relaxing of social codes around visual cultures of sex, the liberalisation of marriage and divorce, the recognition of the enduring impact of childhood sexual violence – it is probably more accurate to suggest that earlier ambivalences have been even further elaborated.

The 1980s North American Sex Wars

In 1980s America, feminist activism was rapidly developing, addressing diverse issues including contraception, breast cancer, marriage, equal pay and abortion. The so-called Sex Wars – a set of verbal and written arguments between feminists – debated how feminists should approach sexuality. The two sides of the wars are often described as 'sex-positive' and 'sex-negative', that is, feminists who wanted to focus on what they perceived as sexual harms or violence and those who wanted to promote sexual freedoms. Pornography was a key element of these disagreements. So-called sex-negative feminists were keen to expose the violence of the pornography industry, while 'sex-positive' feminists wanted to acknowledge both that many women are interested in pornography and that feminist forms of pornography are possible.

Fig. 2 Gayle Rubin's diagram, drawn by Julia Scheele. Originally published in Meg-John Barker and Julia Scheele's book, *Queer: A graphic history*. Reproduced with permission from Julia Scheele.

→ Sexuality and New Technologies

New technologies – most importantly the internet and smart phones – have significantly reshaped scientific, cultural and religious engagements with sexual life.

#MeToo

MeToo was initiated in 2006 by American sexual assault survivor and activist Tarana Burke and quickly became a vast compilation of testimonies about sexual assault, abuse and harassment. The hashtag #MeToo went viral after 2017, when allegations were made by and against famous members of the Hollywood film industry. #MeToo has powerfully underscored the (statistical) normalisation of sexual violence in many parts of the world, bringing issues of sexual harm into public debate and raising ongoing questions about how sexuality should or could be controlled. The idea that people must be able to consent to any sexual practices they are involved in is central to these debates. Feminist research has a lot to say about the complexities of consent in an unequal world.

As is the case in most fields of scientific research, sexual science is burgeoning, facilitated by online publishing and the growth of universities. Pharmaceutical companies are also highly invested in sexual science, and continue to make huge profits from sexuality-related drugs, such as Viagra. The internet and smart phones have also created innumerable places and forms for cultural sexual content: intended to dissuade or condemn, to excite or to explain. The sheer volume of pornographic content now available online would have blown the minds of 1980s feminists, but perhaps the popularity of queer and feminist homemade content may have gladdened some of their hearts. These technologies have created innumerable ways in which anyone with a smart phone can share their sexual experiences, good and bad, and elaborate their desires for public consumption. For feminists oriented towards critique and complaint, for example, this shift has allowed women to speak out about abuses of power and in many cases to translate complaint into legal action. Since 2006, #MeToo has been a powerful force in this respect.

Information and communication technologies like the internet and smart phones have also facilitated other hugely important forms of sexual politics. Using multiple ways of connecting with others, the victims of childhood sexual abuse within the Catholic Church, for example, have been able to bring many perpetrators to justice, and/or to receive apologies and compensation. Unsurprisingly, however, the same technologies can and are used to share misogynous desires and views, to call for hate-filled actions and to complain about feminists' impact on cultural politics and interpersonal relationships. Feminist scholars and activists are doing important work to monitor these movements and to try to hold their members to account. The near ubiquity of smart phones and their availability to ever-younger children has also had a serious impact on how sex education is delivered. Does it make any sense anymore for schools be involved in teaching children about sexuality? Is feminist sexuality education possible today? (See: Sexuality pp.20-21.)

Human sexuality has always been shaped by time and location and is the product of endless encounters of people, ideas and things. Twenty-first-century Euro-American experiences of sexuality have been formed through historical ambivalences about reproduction, morality and the pathologisation of differences. This is perhaps easier to see in retrospect – it is helpful to explore the history of sexuality to come to a rich understanding of our situatedness. But perhaps we could also ponder something that is of our current times. What about, for example, North American feminist sex activists Annie Sprinkle and Beth Stephens' claims about having sex with a river (see textbox on The Ecosex Manifesto)? In Sprinkle and Stephens's activism and performance art, contemporary forms of environmentalism and the importance of nature to our wellbeing enter into and reshape sexual worlds. The politics of sex with robots or with smart phone apps, as in the movies *Bigbug* (2022, dir. Jean-Pierre Jeunet) and *Her* (2013, dir. Spike Jonze), provides another example of contemporary formations of sexuality.

In each example offered in this entry, sexuality appears as both deeply personal and strongly felt but also profoundly of its time and place – that is, social. This complexity makes sexual politics very tricky: there is never a pure or neutral place from which we can condemn or celebrate, or indeed even simply observe, sexuality. We are always, somehow, already in it and of it, which, when you think about it, might be why it's so endlessly interesting.

The Ecosex Manifesto

Ecosex Manifesto 3.0 (2020)
COVID 19 Edit
(i) WE ARE THE
ECOSEXUALS.
The Earth is our lover. We are madly, passionately, and fiercely in love, and we are grateful for this relationship each and every day. In order to create a more mutual and sustainable relationship with the Earth, we collaborate with nature. Covid 19 has reconfirmed these convictions. We garden, we compost, and we are very dirty. Even as we wear masks over our faces and practice social distancing, we stay connected with the human and nonhuman. We treat all sentient and non sentient beings with kindness, respect and affection. We celebrate our E-spots.
(Excerpt from https://sprinklestephens.ucsc.edu/manifestos/)

Is Feminist Sex Education Possible Today?

INTERVIEW WITH MARY LOU RASMUSSEN

Mary Lou Rasmussen is a sexuality education expert, working at the Australian National University. She and Celia Roberts are colleagues and friends. This conversation took place in Canberra, in September 2022.

Celia: So, sex education is usually thought of as a specific curriculum?

Mary Lou: From early childhood, young people are encountering sexuality education at home, at church, online, and it's all across the curriculum at school. It's about what bathrooms you use, what uniform you are asked to wear, your experience in the changing room or what sport you are allowed to play. It's about those erotic feelings you get at school, how you imagine you have to manage those, and how stories are told about sexuality by both teachers and peers. It's about who you can take to the prom or other social events. And it's also about how you talk about gender, sex and sexuality at school outside of the sexuality education curriculum. Can you talk about same-sex marriage, transitioning, being asexual?

Sexuality education often has a specific purpose in mind, namely, to educate people about how they should think about consent and to preserve sexual health through education about sexually transmitted infections. Education that focuses on the vagaries and ambivalences of consent might be more relevant but less achievable. I think that often you can have better conversations about consent outside of sexuality education because sexuality education is often seen as such a fraught space, both for students and for teachers. We tend to put too much emphasis on what happens in the compulsory sexuality education curriculum rather than thinking about all these other sites where sex, gender and sexuality surface at school. There are lots of opportunities for these issues to be explored in a more playful way – in drama, music, history… I think also that the spatiality of schooling is a really big thing to think about – like the playground, how do you deal with young people who are expressing affection at school, for instance? What kind of sexuality education can be put in place there? Do the same rules apply when you've got people who are straight as for young people who are engaged in non-normative relationships? How are schools sending messages about gender when they are encountering students who are non-binary or trans? What are students learning about gender, inclusion and embodiment from the way schools are dealing with those issues?

Celia: That's interesting! Where do sexuality education and gender education intersect? Are they the same thing?

Mary Lou: People often separate out education about gender, sex and sexuality – but for young people, and often for their families and teachers, these things are inseparable in so many ways... Partly due to feminism, the ways young people think about gender have changed a lot. My research project, Queer Generations, has found that the young people born in the 1990s report a large percentage of their peers being out by the end of high school. So, they've actually got a cohort who are queer in some respect, whereas the people who were born in the 1970s often felt like they were the only queer person in their school. There is still isolation, of course, but young people's embrace of fluidity related to gender, sex and sexuality is a significant generational difference we observed.

Young people are hyper-aware that anything they say or do can be captured and replayed, so gender and sexuality are mediated by the fact that they are often being produced in the public domain.

Celia: And do you see less anxiety about being queer? Or less fear at school?

Mary Lou: I think less fear. There is still some anxiety, and that would depend on what your family background is, on cultural and religious issues and on the ongoing existence of homophobia and transphobia in some school contexts – these haven't gone away.

Celia: What about what happens outside of school?

Mary Lou: What happens outside of school permeates schools. There never was any neat division between inside and outside of school, but social media has amplified the intensity and speed of reporting on relationships, and these technologies fold into the school day, often in ways in which young people may have no control.

Celia: What is the role of schools in speaking to students about events that didn't happen at school?

Mary Lou: Your sexuality, gender and identity don't always unfold publicly at the time you want them to. Young people are hyper-aware that anything they say or do can be captured and replayed, so gender and sexuality are mediated by the fact that they are often being produced in the public domain! In the Queer Generations project, people talked about anxieties related to whether they would come out about a relationship or identity status at school. Sometimes that happened without their volition, causing a lot of backlash. People talked about other students in their class knowing that they were queer in some respect before the students themselves knew. In one case, that happened in a sexuality education class where a student asked a teacher, 'Why is so-and-so such a fag?' In that sense, sexuality education can be weaponised. So, unless you've got quite experienced people running it...

> When you talk to young people about their experience of sexuality education at school, they almost uniformly say it was bad, but they wish that it had been better.

Celia: Yes, sex education does seem often to just be given to teachers who may not be the best placed – or even that keen – to do it. Do you think it's better for outside people to come in to deliver that education, or is it better to have people the young students already know bumble through it?

Mary Lou: The research definitely suggests it is better for sexuality education to be delivered by people students know, but the current professional development for teachers in this area is not good, at least in Australia. Here, sexuality education can also be delivered by religious groups, health organisations or by Family Planning associations. This can work well, but there needs to be an opportunity for students to discuss these sessions afterwards with a known teacher.

Celia: So, would you say there's no neutral sex education? It's always got a vision of so-called good sexuality in mind?

Mary Lou: Well, I think it has to! There isn't actually space for it not to because of the constraints of doing it in a school setting. That's why people are making arguments to remove sexuality education from school, because they see it as so fraught. And I really have a lot of sympathy for that position, but I also think it's good for young people to be able to have conversations about sex and sexuality with their peers. When you talk to young people about their experience of sexuality education at school, they almost uniformly say it was bad, but they wish that it had been better. They want opportunities to talk about sexuality, to ask questions and to hear what others in their cohort are thinking about specific issues. For example, we need to have better conversations about porn. Young people are accessing porn, but it's really hard to have a good conversation about that because it is an illegal activity. If these things are forbidden, the only sex education you can have is prohibitive. It's clear that young people are seeking out specific information – one of the young people I talked to in the research said she found an amazing resource on Instagram about how to have an orgasm if you have a vagina. It was very detailed about how to have good sex. This is probably the kind of sexuality education best delivered in the privacy of your own bedroom, or in a group of friends, not at school! We need to think about the best location for education about gender, sex and sexuality.

Suggested resources

Hardy, J. W., & Easton, D. (2017). *The ethical slut: A practical guide to polyamory, open relationships, and other freedoms in sex and love*, Ten Speed Press.

Flo Perry (2020). *How to Have Feminist Sex: A Fairly Graphic Guide*, Particular Books.

Amia Srinivasan (2022). *The Right to Sex: Feminism in the Twenty-First Century*, Picador.

Sex Education (TV series) 2019-present. Netflix, created by Laurie Nunn.

Heartbreak High (TV series reboot), 2002, Netflix, created by Hannah Carroll Chapman.

Bodies

AMBER JAMILLA MUSSER

Bodies are social, locating us in time and place.

Donna Haraway

In *The Cyborg Manifesto* (1985), feminist science studies scholar Donna Haraway argued that the division between nature and culture was artificial and did not take into account the numerous ways that humans have relied on prosthetics such as eyeglasses or walking sticks to help them navigate the world. These adaptations make everyone into a 'cyborg' or cybernetic organism, underscoring just how imbricated people and their cultural environments are.

→ ## Our Bodies, Ourselves

When we think about our bodies, we often think about the ways that bodies are us. Our bodies are where people read identity categories such as race and gender, and each of our bodies' specificities are the result of generational and personal history. Our bodies locate us in time and space, meaning that bodies are profoundly social entities. The way one throws a ball, for example, is the result of specific anatomy as well as gendered and racialised socialisation. But there is a history to this idea of the modern body.

→ ## The Making of the Modern Body

For millennia and across many cultures, the idea of a body was not just about its specific contours, but about how the body connected to broader dimensions – including elemental, spiritual and cosmological forces. It was only in the late seventeenth and the eighteenth centuries that people began to prioritise reason, that the body emerged as a discrete object of study related to the individual. This shift had profound consequences. Marking the distinction between body and environment enabled people to imagine bodies as their own organisational systems, subordinate to the mind, to be managed. In philosopher René Descartes's famous proclamation 'I think therefore I am', for example, the body is rendered inferior to the mind. In addition to emphasising the importance of will, this ordering reflects a devaluation of the body such that those who were more closely associated with the physicality of sex or other bodily activities like eating were described as primitive, and as bodies who did not or could not conform to discipline; those whose bodies bled or leaked, or whose capacities differed, were thus regarded as weaker and more in need of external control. The presumption that some groups of people required management because of bodily differences is one of the paternalistic rationales for colonialism and slavery.

Jim Crow

Jim Crow refers to the discriminatory practices of segregation and anti-Blackness that were pervasive throughout the United States following the abolition of slavery. Laws enacted to prevent racial intermingling relegated Black people to positions of inferiority. Jim Crow is said to have ended with the civil rights movement in the 1960s.

→ Bodies and Regulation

There is a contemporary legacy to this racialised and gendered classification of people. We might think, for example, of the various forms of prejudice based on appearance. When someone is imagined to be less capable of performing an action or if their actions are considered unintelligent because of the way that they look – consider the history of discriminatory anti-Black hiring practices or even the stereotypes around blondes – we can recognise forms of racism, sexism, ableism and fatphobia. These types of prejudice have also been legally enshrined based on the presumption that some people should not have control over their own bodies. This is apparent in histories of the state sterilising people with mental illness or those with 'enough children', or, even more scandalously, those on welfare in order to prevent them from having children. In some of these cases, people were not even made aware of these interventions. These impulses to control others based on a hierarchy of bodies and their presumed capacities make clear the stakes of bodily autonomy. Instead of navigating these different forms of prejudice and authority, what would it look like to have people decide what to do with their own bodies?

The Black South African runner disqualified because of gender ruling.

In 2009, Black South African runner Caster Semenya won gold at the Twelfth International Amateur Athletic Federation World Championships in Berlin. Instead of accolades, however, her wide margin of victory and quick personal improvement prompted intense scrutiny. Since some assumed she might be taking testosterone to enhance her performance, she was asked to submit to tests for sex verification. Whilst those results were never publicised, Semenya was permitted to keep running. Eventually, it was leaked that Semenya was assigned female at birth, but born intersex, which means that her sex was not determinable. (See: Trans p.70.) A previous ruling by the IAAF permitted those with naturally elevated levels of testosterone, like Semenya, to continue to compete because it could not be ascertained whether testosterone produced a measurable difference in athletic performance.

Although Semenya continued to compete, she was haunted by various controversies involving her hormone levels. Her success on the track meant that she was again (falsely) suspected of doping and the IAAF debated the fairness of having athletes like Semenya, with more testosterone, compete against other women. Finally, in 2016, the IAAF changed their policy to disallow athletes from competing unless their hormone levels fell within a certain range for the specific distances in which Semenya competed – meaning that Semenya and others like her would have had to take drugs to reduce their body's production of testosterone. Semenya challenged this ruling, arguing that it narrowly defined who could be considered a woman, and additionally asserting that taking these drugs would produce unknown effects. As a result of the ruling, Semenya did not compete in the 2020 Tokyo Olympics.

In Semenya's story, we see the reinforcement of the gender binary – that men are different from women – and gender norms – there is only one way to be a woman (see: Sex/Gender pp.10-11).

Despite scientific disagreement about what determines gender – genitalia, genes or hormones – Semenya's body was determined to fall outside of the conventions for female bodies. Some of this has to do with her hormone levels, but we might also consider the ways that Semenya's race (Black women have historically been seen as less feminine) and her sexuality (Semenya came out as queer and married her female partner in 2015) contributed to these attempts to argue that Semenya is not a woman and to discipline her body so that it would conform to an idealised standard of femininity. Semenya's body, in other words, became a focal point for debates about the line between exceptional athletic performance and what constitutes the acceptable limits of femaleness and thus femininity. Moreover, in this scrutiny of Semenya's body, we can see extensions of colonial and racist forms of discipline and punishment which would regard Semenya as not capable of managing her body – hence the athletic governing board having to grant her permission to run as a woman regardless of her own feelings on the matter. In July 2023, Caster Semenya won her appeal at the European Court of Human Rights (ECHR), which ruled that she had been discriminated against and commented that there were 'serious questions' about the current World Athletics regulations' validity.

Semenya's body became a focal point for debates about the line between exceptional athletic performance and what constitutes the acceptable limits of femaleness and thus femininity.

Suggested reading

Sporting Gender: The History, Science and Stories of Transgender and Intersex Athletes by Joanna Harper and David Epstein (Rowan and Littlefield, 2019)

WIKIMEDIA COMMONS/CHELL HILL

More than merely managing bodily functions, bathrooms regulate bodies.

Bathrooms are key sites to consider how bodies are managed, since they are public places where people attend to intimate activities. One of the most frequent and visible ways that bathrooms enact social segregation is through gender specificity. In the absence of gender-neutral or individual toilets, men's and women's toilets are separated. This has resulted in a dearth of changing tables for babies in men's rooms, due to assumptions about family structures and caretaking, and strict policing of who is permitted to enter women's restrooms because women, more than men, are presumed to require the toilet to function as a safe space. In this context, safe space designates an area free from the possibility of violence, largely from men. Unfortunately, this idea of a safe space has made bathrooms very policed sites. We see this when masculine-presenting women, and gender non-binary people face difficulties when attempting to use women's toilets and, especially, in the continued legal attempts to ban trans women from these spaces – despite the increased danger that they would likely face in using men's bathrooms (see: Trans p.70).

Battles over trans people using restrooms is just a more recent incarnation in the long history of bathrooms, bodies and containment.

Battles over trans people using restrooms, however, is just a more recent incarnation in the long history of bathrooms, bodies and containment. In the United States during the Jim Crow era, bathrooms (and water fountains) were famously segregated, with separate facilities for Black and white people. Whilst fear is also at the root of this separation, what is at stake is the fear of contamination. People supporting segregated bathrooms argued that there might be something essentially different and dangerous about Black people that should not be encountered in the intimate, ostensibly vulnerable, space of the bathroom.

Separate toilets enabled the belief in biological racial differences to persist and were also an attempt to prevent intimate racial mixing. In a related vein, bathrooms have also been used to enact colonial disciplining, promoting assimilation and the adoption of particular cultural norms which were imagined to be cleaner and less primitive than others. During the US occupation of the Philippines, for example, the government replaced squat toilets with Western ones in the hopes of shifting people's bathroom comportment into something that was perceived to be more modern and hygienic. Finally, because of their invitation to intimacy and privacy, bathrooms have also historically been sites of homosexual cruising. In moments when homosexuality was publicly policed and many men were closeted, the sex segregation and privacy afforded by toilets enabled men to meet and even offered physical space for clandestine sexual encounters. Here, we might think about the creative ways that people have subverted forms of spatial discipline to find pleasure.

DAN BRUNSDON / THE NOUN PROJECT

Queer

AMBER JAMILLA MUSSER

An expansive term, queer describes a range of non-heterosexual identities.

→ From Act to Identity

The modern conception of sexual identity did not exist before the late nineteenth century, when scientists became interested in attempting to catalogue different forms of sexual deviance (see: Sexuality p.20). Before this interest in defining sexual norms and perversions, people's sexual behaviours were not considered part of their identities. A man might be sexually compelled by another man, for example, but this did not earn him the label of 'homosexual'. There was a division between identity and action. As the nineteenth century wore on, however, there was a shift from understanding actions as deviant to understanding that these desires constituted the central part of someone's identity.

→ The Changing Politics of 'Deviance'

The term queer has not always been synonymous with lesbian, gay or other LGBTQIAA+ identity. When it was first used in the English language, it meant peculiar or odd – counterfeit money, for example, was described as queer. It wasn't until the mid-twentieth century that the term was applied to people, and then it was often used as a derogatory term for homosexuals. In response to the AIDS emergency and the subsequent villanisation of gay people, activists began to use the term queer to signal their unwillingness to live with the status quo. In the mid-1980s, groups such as ACT UP (AIDS Coalition to Unleash Power) and its offshoot, Queer Nation, began agitating for more research on HIV and AIDS and better treatment for gay people. Their use of queer signalled a politics of nonconformity. These groups appropriated the connotations of deviance to critique the violence that dominant norms produce and to indicate a desire to produce better and more just conditions for everyone.

→ Too Inclusive?

In some ways, however, the explicit reclamation of the term queer drained it of some of its political charge and even radicalness. In addition to becoming shorthand for any type of non-normative identity, the word also became a way to describe unconventional behaviour more broadly. People who stay up all night, those who live in communal housing and those who enjoy recreational drugs might all be described as queer because their comportment does not align with the dominant values of a capitalist society that valorise productivity and achievement. However, some activists, especially those based in countries outside of the United States, argue that queer and queerness are terms and ideas that have been externally imposed on people and places as signs of modernity without paying attention to the particularities of their specific histories and political movements. In other words, queer itself becomes a site of cultural imperialism, or cultural domination, in its erasure of local practices and ways of knowing.

CUIR

In response to the tensions embedded in the word queer, activists in the Americas have begun to use the word 'cuir' to highlight the local specificities of non-normative identities and to demarcate decolonial possibilities for sexuality that, for example, do not revolve around a gender binary and which might work with Indigenous understandings of intimacy.

An Umbrella Term

When people describe themselves as queer, they are usually identifying themselves as a member of the LGBTQIAA+ community. In this case, queer does not specify any particular sexual orientation, other than a departure from monogamous heterosexuality, which is understood as synonymous with gender and sexual normativity. In this usage, queer functions as an umbrella term that includes all who wish to align themselves with non-normativity. It is applied to both sexual orientation and gender identity, with people who identify as genderqueer, for example, often refusing to adhere to conventions of femininity or masculinity.

 **Queer Coalition**

Practices of coalition forge political alternatives to state neglect.

One of the most famous events in US queer history – the 1969 Stonewall riots – offers testament to the power of a queer coalition. Fed up with police harassment, which was legal because homosexuality was illegal, and during one of the recurrent police raids on the Stonewall Inn, a gay and lesbian bar in Greenwich Village in New York City, patrons like Marsha P. Johnson and Sylvia Rivera, members of the Street Transvestite Action Revolutionaries (STAR), began to fight back by throwing bricks and assaulting the police. Soon, other drag queens, lesbians and gay men joined the fray. People came together despite their differences – everyone had their own relationship to police presence and their own motivation for protesting – but it was this unity that shifted the landscape of queer rights in the US by making a queer community visible and political. One of the powerful things about a queer coalition is that it shows how broad a movement can be and how people with different interests can still work together to attain common goals.

We are in a different historical moment than Stonewall, however, and queerness is no longer as firmly attached to sexuality. Now, our challenge is how to bring together the idea of queer as sexual identity with queer as non-normative in order to show how different identities might share points of connection that have nothing to do with sexuality.

One might imagine, for example, a coalition between queer activists, Black LGBT people and 'welfare queens', the derogatory term used to describe and demonise single mothers (presumed to be Black) who are perceived to be receiving too many benefits from the state. In addition to broadening ideas of queerness to include heterosexuality, we can see that racialisation and its historical legacies produce their own deviations from normativity and their own versions of queerness. What we also see is that, as a result, queerness does not necessarily reside in individual identifications or identities, but rather in a

shared alienated relationship from the state that leaves each of these figures more vulnerable to exclusion. Queer coalition suggests that understanding these connections might produce more unexpected insight into what constitutes state violence, as well as inviting new strategies to produce structural change.

In lieu of focusing on the needs or desires of individuals, queer coalitions look to the ways that governments (for example) make it difficult for certain populations to access rights. Thinking coalitionally, this question of access resonates with disability justice activists, immigration activists and prison activists. Each of these groups has their own perspective on questions of access, but we can see how the issue gains depth when these different interest groups come together in the name of queer coalition.

Suggested Resources

Cohen, Cathy. 'Punks, Bull-daggers, and Welfare Queens: The Radical Potential of Queer Politics?' GLQ 3, no. 4 (1997): 437–465.

Is there an underside to some countries' promotion of sexual diversity?

Once homosexuality became more culturally accepted, a landscape of rights began to open up – including that of marriage, adoption and military service. In other words, homosexuality was no longer seen as something that prevented one from enjoying the rights and privileges of being a citizen. In fact, in tandem with this broadening of rights, the acceptance and valorisation of homosexuality also became a sign that one's nation was progressive and modern. Homonationalism is the term for these forms of alliance between the nation and homosexuality.

Countries that did not explicitly support LGBTQ rights were seen as less modern, and the defence of sexual minorities was used as an excuse to invade other countries. As an example of how this rhetoric circulated culturally, we can look at the portrayal of Saddam Hussein in the cartoon South Park, where he is shown as irrational and sexually repressed – the 'joke' being that Hussein's repression of sexual minorities was itself an indication that there was something inherently sexually pathological about him. The implication was that the US invasion of Iraq would be sexually liberatory for him and other Iraqis. Notice, however, that the emphasis on Iraq as needing to be sexually liberated camouflages the violence of invasion, which includes the destruction of local forms of activism, alongside a focus on Western sexual norms.

Relatedly, there is also the phenomenon of 'pink washing' – when a nation's public embrace of sexual minorities, often through the promotion of LGBTQ tourism, is also used as a way to signal its modernity and its alliance with the US, which can then serve to hide the poor treatment of racial and ethnic minorities within its borders. As an example of this, we might think about the fact that South Africa made marriage between same-sex couples legal back in 2006, yet Black South African lesbians face high rates of 'corrective rape' and murder. We might also think about the fact that Israel throws one of the largest Pride parades in the world, has policies that make it easier for LGBTQ families to have and raise children and supports marriage for same-sex couples – all this whilst those who live on the Gaza Strip face shortages of electricity and healthcare and violence at the hands of the Israeli army. 'Pink washing' is a term that allows one to see how promoting LGBTQ equality can be used to occlude the ways that intersections of race, sexuality and gender render some people more vulnerable to violence than others.

What these different relationships between homosexuality and the state point us towards is the ways that queer is not synonymous with homosexuality or, indeed, any sexual identity. Moreover, not conforming to dominant ideals, sexual identity or behaviour – queer or otherwise – is not automatically liberatory or political. In showing different ways that homosexuality can be and has been recuperated by the state, we can also think about different ways that queerness might resist this incorporation and maintain its more radical political edge.

Suggested Resources

Cohen, Cathy. 'Punks, Bull-daggers, and Welfare Queens: The Radical Potential of Queer Politics?' GLQ 3, no. 4 (1997): 437–465.

Race and Ethnicity

SIMIDELE DOSEKUN

Race and ethnicity are socially created ways of categorising, and very often judging, different groups of people.

Suggested reading

W. E. B Du Bois
The Souls of Black Folk, 1903
An African American sociologist who argued that the major 'problem of the twentieth century is the problem of the color-line', meaning racism, racist violence and racist segregation. Du Bois also proposed the idea that racially oppressed people come to have a 'double consciousness' or dual sense of self because, as a result of their subordinate position, they become able to see themselves 'through the eyes of others'.

Race and ethnicity are social categories. They are ways of categorising and identifying and, ultimately, valuing or devaluing different groups of people according to actual or assumed traits and origins that they share. Race generally refers to people's physical, phenotypical features such as skin colour and hair texture, whilst ethnicity refers to their history, culture, traditions, language and so on. Any given racial group encompasses many ethnic groups. For instance, most Africans belong to the racial group typically called 'Black', and to thousands of different ethnic groups.

→ Human-Made but Very Real

Race and ethnicity may appear natural. Race, especially, may look like the most natural and obvious of things, an aspect of identity and belonging that everyone just has from birth and that we often think we can read right off people's bodies, based on how they look, and that does not change. Race is like sex in this regard (see: Sex/Gender p.10). In reality, race and ethnicity are not natural entities, but social constructs. This means that they are categories invented or constructed and made meaningful in and by society. It means that they are *human-made*. This is not to say that these categories are therefore unreal. Race and ethnicity are real because we have made them real. We organise our societies around these categories, and on a personal level many people identify

deeply with their given racial or ethnic identities and groups. We live by these social constructs – indeed, people even lose their lives because of them. So even though, at root, race and ethnicity are social and cultural fictions, they are very real in effect. They are also very real in the ways in which they come to intersect or work in tandem with other social categories such as gender, sexuality and class (see: Intersectionality p.50).

→ The Origins of Race

Race as we know it today is a modern invention. Many consider that this invention was tied to European impe-rialism, including the transatlantic slave trade, as a way of justifying oppression. The modern construction of race was initially based on beliefs that different groups of people, from different parts of the world, possess innate and fixed biological properties that determine not only their outward appearance but also their inner attributes, such as their moral character, intellectual abilities and even basic humanity and worth. Science – or, really, what today we would consider *pseudoscience* – was mobilised to find evidence of race, and more importantly evidence of racial hierarchies: heads and other body parts were measured, experiments were conducted, cadavers were dissected, to try to prove that we are not equally human. The evidence was never found because it does not exist.

Cultural Racism

Nowadays, we're not so likely to hear racism expressed or justified in crude biological terms. Instead, racist sentiments and ideas tend to be expressed more subtly, in terms of the so-called culture or ways of living of different racial groups. For example: 'they just don't appreci-ate the value of education'; 'they tend to be quite lazy'; 'they have too many babies'; 'they are just different from us'.

Suggested reading

Edward W. Said

Orientalism, 1978

A Palestinian literary scholar who argued that British and French imperial societies have a history of depicting and imagining the places they called 'the Orient', India and the Arab world especially, in racist and stereotypical ways: as 'exotic' and 'romantic' but also 'barbaric'. Said called this system of knowledge and representation 'orientalism'.

→ Racism and Ethnic Chauvinism

Racism is a system of domination and oppression based on ideas and constructs of race. It includes everything from beliefs that one or more racial groups are superior to others, to race-based discrimination, violence and hatred, to the organisation of societies and economies, even physical space, along racial lines. Incidentally, the word 'racism' was the source of inspiration for the coining of the feminist keyword 'sexism', which refers to a system of domination and oppression based on sex and gender. Ethnic chauvinism or bigotry refers to the same kinds of attitudes, systems and processes in relation to ethnicity, and is very common in multi-ethnic societies.

Racism and ethnic chauvinism have long been and, unfortunately, continue to be the cause of grave injustices and violence around the world: the transatlantic slave trade and the ensuing system of chattel slavery, the Holocaust, genocide in Rwanda and other such mass atrocities, apartheid in South Africa, and forced dispossession of land in so many places. The list is almost endless.

MIKE VON/UNSPLASH

→ Fighting Racism

Racism is deeply ingrained in many societies and cultures. It is embedded in laws and policies, in institutional norms, in the kinds of images and values that powerful media propagate, and in everyday and even unconscious attitudes and behaviours. How can it be challenged then? How can we dismantle racism?

Firstly we need to develop a deep understanding of what racism is, the myriad ways in which it manifests, and the social and political interests and agendas that it serves. For instance, it is important to understand that an action, statement or policy can be racist in effect, in terms of what it does or engenders, or how it is received, even if this is not the intention. Relatedly, we need to understand the concept of institutional racism so that we know that we need to look for racism not just in the overt policies or profile of an institution, but also in the habits and unspoken rules of the place. We also need to understand the history of our societies, to grasp how and why it is that different racial groups have come to be positioned as they are.

To fight racism, it is not enough for people to be 'not racist' personally or individually, or to claim that they are colourblind, meaning that they do not see race. Pretending that race does not matter or that we do not notice it, or that we are not personally implicated, does not solve the problem of racism, it only denies it. To fight racism, we all need to be actively anti-racist. Among other things, this means we must keep an eye out for racism, and to recognise and call it out when we see it. It also means that we must acknowledge the ways in which we may enact or perpetuate racism, or benefit from racist dynamics in the world, even when we do not necessarily mean to. We also need to be ready and humble enough to listen to those who experience racism, to try to understand more about the problem.

Institutional Racism

In 1999, an inquiry into how the London Metropolitan Police had handled its investigation of the murder of Stephen Lawrence, a young Black British man, concluded that the force was 'institutionally racist'. To say that an organisation is institutionally racist is to say that the way the organisation works, how things are designed and how things tick along, the patterns of employment, the culture of the place and so on have racist logics and consequences, even if or when all these things look neutral. The concept of institutional racism is particularly useful to help us understand that if racism persists in any given institution, it is not just because of racist individuals or 'a few bad apples'; rather, the problem is much more deeply embedded. It exists in the norms and in the very fabric of the institution.

Beauty and race are deeply entangled because both have to do with values and judgements attached to what people look like.

The popular saying claims that beauty is in the eye of the beholder, but if we stop and really think about this, it is clearly not the case when it comes to human beauty – and many other forms of beauty as well. Most societies have dominant visions and standards about the kinds of physical appearances and traits that are considered beautiful or not, and what kinds of people fit the bill. These standards shift over time.

Media are a key site in which we can see the predominant ideas of beauty that hold sway in a society at any given moment. The point is that beauty is rarely a matter of personal or idiosyncratic taste. It is social and historical and cultural.

Skin colour and tone tend to matter very much in the social construction of beauty, along with other racialised traits like hair texture, or the shape, size and relative proportions of facial features and other body parts. In short, beauty standards are racialised and often racist. And of course, beauty standards also very much gendered, so they are a clear instance where we see race and sex/gender, and racism and sexism, intersecting.

In white-dominant societies, it is white bodies and physical features most associated with whiteness that tend to be vaunted and represented as the most beautiful, especially for women. In many other places – India, Japan or Korea, say – it is a fair or pale complexion that is generally considered most beautiful, because fairer skin has a historical association with more privileged social classes who do not have to carry out manual labour in the sun.

'Black is beautiful' became a rallying cry during the Black and anti-colonial nationalist movements in the 1960s. It was an impassioned call for Black people to embrace their bodies and looks, to reject and resist long-standing racist representations of Blackness – and features associated with it, such as Afro hair – as unattractive.

↓ | Colourism

Colourism is a form of prejudice or discrimination based on differences in skin tone, in which lighter tones are privileged or preferred over darker ones. Colourism is related to but differs from racism in that it includes discrimination *within* a racial group, including by members of the group itself. Colourism is when, for example, Black or brown people systematically prefer or consider lighter-skinned members of their groups as the most beautiful or esteemed. It is when people, most typically women, are put under pressure to lighten their skin tone or to avoid getting a tan, to try to stay as fair as possible. In white-dominant societies, women of colour are under-represented in mainstream media, but of these women those who are darker-skinned are even less represented or visible than their lighter counterparts. This is another instantiation of colourism. Colourism affects people in many spheres of their lives, including their education and employment prospects, their dating and marriage prospects and potentially their self-esteem.

A whole section of the cosmetics industry is motivated by and continues to feed colourism, with products and services that promise to lighten skin, straighten hair and so on. The skin-lightening industry alone was estimated to be worth about $4 billion in 2020.

→ Crossing Racial and Ethnic Lines

As racial and ethnic categories are created by society rather than natural, it becomes possible for people to try to move across them.

Blackface

'Blackface' refers to the practice in which people who are not Black, typically white people, smear black substances such as shoe polish on their faces as a form of supposed entertainment, play and dress up. It is associated with minstrelsy in particular, a historic genre of theatrical performance that emerged during the time of the enslavement of Black people in North America, in which highly offensive, cartoonish stereotypes about them were enacted for white audiences by white performers dressed in blackface. Dressing in blackface is also the sort of thing people do for Halloween, to this day. The practice is considered highly offensive because of its racist history and connotations.

In 2015, an American woman, Rachel Dolezal, who presented herself and was perceived by many as Black, was revealed to be white. The truth of Dolezal's racial identity came to light when her white parents spoke to the media about who their daughter really was. As the scandal unfolded, it was revealed that Dolezal had invented a Black father and accompanying backstory for herself, regularly used tanning products to darken the appearance of her skin, and wore wigs and braids to camouflage the true texture of her hair. Dolezal was subject to widespread criticism, mockery and ostracism, and ended up losing her job. She was accused of engaging in a form of blackface, of treating Blackness like an exotic commodity or accessory.

Much more common than white people attempting to live and be seen as members of a different racial group are attempts by members of subordinated racial groups to move into the category of whiteness because it is socially advantageous for them to do so. When South Africa was under apartheid rule, for instance, the population was strictly segregated into four main racial categories, of which 'white' was at the apex and 'Black' was at the base, with 'coloured', meaning mixed race, and 'Indian' in the middle. One's official racial categorisation determined almost all aspects of one's life and opportunities: the kinds and quality of schools one could attend, the neighbourhoods in which one could or could not live, how much liberty one had to move around the country, whom one could marry and so on. In this situation, there were many incentives for those who could to try to pass as white, to enjoy the social privileges of whiteness.

↓ | **Passing**

'Passing' refers to a practice in which an individual attempts to present themselves to society as a member of a racial group other than their own, and to be duly seen and treated as such. People may try to pass in temporary situations, or they may try to live permanently in this way. Passing can also be thought of as 'racial masquerade', a practice of hiding one's true face, and self, behind a costume, a façade. Passing is possible precisely because race is a social construct rather than a biological or natural fact, and because race relies heavily on visual and other exterior markers. When people are able to pass successfully (whether temporarily or permanently), it is basically because they are able to play and look the part. They are able to 'do' the race with which they wish to be associated. They may be able to pass just as they are, or they may need to tweak or manage certain aspects of their physical appearance: straightening their hair, say, or using makeup lighter or darker than their own skin tone, or avoiding the sun. As in the case of Rachel Dolezal, to try to pass on a permanent basis necessarily involves creating a new tale of who one is and where one comes from, which, almost by definition, involves hiding or even cutting ties with one's family and community of origin, as these will give the game away. In short, passing comes with a high personal and psychological cost.

Nella Larsen
***Passing*, 1929**
Passing is a 1929 novel by Nella Larsen which tells of two Black women in 1920s Harlem who are light-skinned enough to pass as white. One of the women takes the option to pass and ends up married to a racist white man; the other does not and remains in her Black community. It is a tale of the complex entanglement of race, gender and sexuality in a deeply segregated and racist society, and reveals the many personal costs and losses of living a life of racial masquerade. In 2021, the book was adapted into a film by Netflix.

Intersectionality

SIMIDELE DOSEKUN

Social systems of oppression intersect and multiply and compound one another in complex ways.

The Combahee River Collective Statement

This is a 1977 statement published by a Black lesbian socialist feminist collective in Boston in which they outline a vision for justice and liberation from intersectional oppressions. As the women explain in the statement, for them, the fact that 'racial, sexual, heterosexual, and class oppression' combine and work together is not merely an abstract or theoretical idea. *It is the very condition of their lives.* Hence in the statement they express a commitment to understanding and fighting against all these forces simultaneously.

→ What is Intersectionality?

'Intersectionality' refers to the fact that social systems of power and oppression like sexism, racism, class and imperialism do not operate in isolation but rather intersect – converge, overlap, combine and so on – and in so doing compound and intensify one another. Another way we can think about it is that intersectionality refers to the fact that when people find themselves placed by society at the sharp end of multiple systems of power, the result for them is *multidimensional* situations and experiences of oppression. Black women, for instance, contend systematically with sexism and racism, and often class oppression as well. It is fair to say that for most women the world over, sexism is not the only system of power and injustice that they face, at the same time that it factors into their experiences of other such systems.

Kimberlé Crenshaw, 2018.
HEINRICH-BÖLL-STIFTUNG /
MOHAMED BADARNE / FLICKR

→ A Black Feminist Knowledge Tradition

The particular term 'intersectionality' was coined in 1989 by an African American feminist legal scholar, Kimberlé Crenshaw. But the concept or idea that the term represents, and the type of understanding of the world that it proposes, has a long history. It comes out of a Black feminist intellectual and activist tradition, which itself is based upon Black women's lived experiences at the intersections of racism and sexism especially. This includes experiences of being pushed by racism to the margins of feminism and pushed by sexism to the margins of Black civil rights and nationalist struggles.

Before Intersectionality

Before Kimberlé Crenshaw coined the term 'intersectionality', other African American feminist thinkers and writers had proposed similar concepts and terms to conceptualise and characterise the situation of Black women in America.

These include the idea that Black women face the 'double jeopardy' (Frances Beale) of being Black and female, the 'multiple jeopardy' (Deborah King) of sexism, racism and class oppression, and the notion that they live in a systematically organised 'matrix of domination' (Patricia Hill Collins) made up of 'interlocking' oppressions (the Combahee River Collective).

→

Feminism: Intersectional or Bullshit?

'Demarginalising the Intersection of Sex and Race'

This is a 1989 legal academic article in which Kimberlé Crenshaw first proposed the term 'intersectionality'. Crenshaw discusses a number of court cases that different groups of Black women in America had brought forward, in which they alleged that they had faced discrimination at work not just for being women or Black, but precisely for being both of these things at once. In all the cases, the court was unable to recognise or know how to deal with the intersectionality of the women's experiences and claims. The legal standard for sex discrimination is effectively that of white women's experiences, Crenshaw argues, whilst the standard for racial discrimination is effectively that of Black men's experiences. Black women fall through the cracks.

Intersectionality has major implications for feminism. First of all, the concept helps us to understand that not only are there differences between women because of how they are positioned in society in terms of categories such as race and class, but there are also power relations between them. The fact is that some women are always among the beneficiaries of the very systems and forces in society that oppress other women. Take the historical system of slavery in the Americas. White women benefitted in many ways from the enslavement of Black women (and men) and exercised power over them, even though they were oppressed themselves on the basis of their gender and unequal to white men.

Intersectionality debunks any notion that women make up a single, natural or necessarily united constituency *as* women. And with this, it illuminates the fact that there is no such thing as a single or universal feminism that simply exists or operates on behalf of all women. Think again about the example of slavery. Clearly it would be impossible to say that in this situation Black and white women could or would have united around anything like women's issues, rights or interests. Not only were these sets of women worlds apart, their basic interests were fundamentally opposed.

Intersectionality helps us to see that feminism as a political project and feminists as people are not immune to the many ills and injustices of their societies: racism, class exploitation, homophobia, transphobia and so on. It shows, also, that these kinds of issues are necessarily feminist issues too because they impact the lives of differently positioned women.

In 2011, a Latina feminist writer, Flavia Dzodan, came up with the expression 'My feminism will be intersectional or it will be bullshit.' Her point was simply that feminism is not good enough if it does not pay attention to intersectionality.

→ Towards Intersectional Solidarity

Political solidarity is when different groups of people or political movements which do not have an obvious shared identity or set of immediate interests actively decide to band together and support one another in pursuit of their respective causes because they see these causes as united or connected under a larger shared vision of social justice. It is when a group decides to become an ally to another. Because different systems of oppression and therefore different forms of social injustice are interconnected, as the concept of intersectionality tells us, solidarity becomes all the more necessary and important as a political goal and practice. It means an attempt and commitment to fight interconnected oppressions together, at the same time, and to support people and groups who suffer injustice in different ways, including ways that may be far removed from our own experience.

Solidarity has to be built and achieved and defended, it cannot be simply assumed or taken for granted. It is hard, even discomfiting work. It entails fostering connections with people and groups with whom one may not have much in common; consistently being reflexive or mindful about power dynamics that may exist or emerge in the larger group, and being ready to tackle them; being willing to listen and learn from others, and to accept critique of our own positions or practices where necessary; investing time, energy, possibly money and other resources into other people's struggles, and so on.

Because different systems of oppression and therefore different forms of social injustice are interconnected, as the concept of intersectionality tells us, solidarity becomes all the more necessary and important as a political goal and practice.

A Tool for Thinking Intersectionally

Question	The Short Answer
The concept of intersectionality was proposed by a Black woman and it comes out of the Black feminist knowledge tradition. Does this mean that intersectionality is only about or for Black women? Can we apply it to other kinds of women or would this be a kind of appropriation?	It is important to understand and acknowledge the origins of the concept of intersectionality in Black feminism. But the concept is not owned by Black feminism or only relevant or applicable to Black women. Nor is intersectionality only about the intersecting of sexism and racism. We can apply the concept of intersectionality wherever we see systems of power and oppression converging and compounding in people's lives.
Doesn't intersectionality needlessly divide feminism by dividing women? How will women advance feminist causes if they are not united?	Intersectionality is not about splintering feminism or causing or magnifying divisions between women. Quite the contrary: whilst it may be difficult or uncomfortable to see or admit that there are all kinds of tensions and inequalities between women and between feminists, doing so actually strengthens feminism in the end. Thinking about intersectionality helps us to see how much gets brushed under the carpet if we assume or pretend that feminism is simply a united camp, or a movement about what Kimberlé Crenshaw calls a 'single-axis' struggle against sexism or gender-based oppression only. It shows us how much work feminists have to do, that we have to fight all systems of oppression wherever we see them and that we also have to actively foster alliances and solidarities between different kinds of women if we are ever really to achieve social justice.

Question

The word 'intersectionality' seems to be everywhere these days. Are we all obliged to use the word now? Do I have to call myself an 'intersectional feminist'? What are we supposed to do with intersectionality, practically speaking?

$\rightarrow$

The Short Answer

It certainly looks like intersectionality has become fashionable within feminism of late – although, on the flipside, intersectionality is also something of an anti-feminist talking point for some people, used to whip up anger and fear!

To be a feminist who takes intersectionality seriously, it is not necessary to use the literal word or to name or declare oneself 'an intersectional feminist'. And even if one is doing these things, it's possible to be missing the point a little.

Intersectionality is not about advocating for or celebrating diversity. It is not about personal identities or a requirement for feminists to individually name or acknowledge all their own social positions, along the lines of 'I am a white, cisgender, straight woman'. It also isn't supposed to be an easy or politically virtuous label to stick onto things.

The most apt way to understand intersectionality is that it is a *tool* for thinking in and about feminism. It offers a way of understanding the world and prompts us to ask certain kinds of questions: about the multiple facets of different women's experiences, about the many things that unite and divide women, about feminism and what it is or needs to be about, about who gets to speak in the name of feminism. In short, intersectionality prompts us to think in more complex ways about power relations, including power relations within feminism.

→ Systems of Power and Oppression

Intersectionality is about the interweaving of different systems of power and oppression, but what are *these* exactly?

↓ Social Stratification

All societies are stratified in many ways, meaning that people are divided into different and unequal or hierarchically organised categories and groupings. Finding yourself in one social category or another unjustly affects your life experiences and life chances. It affects the kinds of rights and opportunities that you will or will not have, where you start out (and often also where you end up) on the socioeconomic ladder, whether or not you can freely and openly love and sexually desire the way that you want, whether you are likely to be respected by society or looked down upon. And much more.

Social stratifications that we commonly find in societies around the world include those of sex and gender, sexuality, race, ethnicity and caste, religion, class, and ability and disability. At a global level, there are also divisions between more- and less-powerful nations.

↓ From Petty Prejudices to Institutional Frameworks

When we talk about systems of power and oppression, we are referring to all the factors and forces that create, maintain and justify unequal and unfair social stratifications, all the things that add up to mean that, systematically, some social groups are more powerful and privileged, whilst others are more disadvantaged and oppressed. Systems of power and oppression are made up of and sustained by everything from the ideas and prejudices that people hold or are taught about social groups different from their own, to the different ways in which people treat others whom they consider to be like them and those they deem different, to how the economic, political, cultural and legal institutions of a society are designed and operate, including their informal or unspoken rules.

Economics are a major factor. In almost all cases, the most powerful and privileged groups in a society are those who have the most ability to gain and to maintain economic advantage for themselves (see: Class p.60).

↓ Oppression

To be oppressed literally means to be 'pressed down'. The feminist philosopher Iris Marion Young proposed that a social group is oppressed if the general experience of members of that social group includes one or more of five conditions. One: their labour is exploited, which is to say they are not adequately or fairly compensated for the work that they do. Two: they are socially marginalised, or, in other words, they are pushed to the edges of society. Three: they lack authority and status in society. Four: their culture is devalued and they are stereotyped. Five: they face systematic violence.

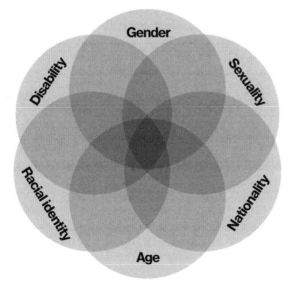

Fig. 3 Intersectionality

Even taking into account their different intersectional positions, all women face oppression in some if not most of the above ways in male-dominant societies. Here are some examples: The labour that women do in the home and to take care of children and the elderly is typically undervalued by society, and not just when it is unpaid but also when it is paid (see: Work p.124). Men's perspectives dominate society, men run the most important institutions and they are considered to hold the most authority. And then of course there is the fact of violence of all sorts against women, which is endemic.

↓ | Privilege

The word 'privilege' is mobilised a lot these days: 'male privilege', 'white privilege', 'heterosexual privilege', etc. It is referring to social privilege. Social privilege means the advantages that people have in some or possibly many respects or domains of their lives simply because they belong to one social group versus another in a society in which different groups are unequally placed. People tend to be unaware of their privilege; they take it for granted because it is what they know and because they likely have never experienced or had to think about the absence of it. On this note, we can also understand the concept of privilege as referring to the fact that some people never or rarely have to think about, much less experience, various forms of inequality and injustice that are routine for others. For some people, getting stopped by the police is not a big deal, for example, whilst for others it is a fearful situation, even a life-or-death one.

To say someone experiences a particular form of privilege does not mean that they have a rosy life with no problems or no social disadvantages at all. It just means pointing to some particular type or domain of advantage that they have – due to the way in which they are positioned with regards to relations of powers – that others lack systematically. If a man is disadvantaged by his race or class status, for example, to say he has male privilege is not to discount or deny these disadvantages, it is simply to say that he is not disadvantaged by gender or sex as well.

↓ Compounding Oppressions

Often, many systems of social stratification and systems of oppressions are layered on top of each other or, again, intersecting. They meet and they work through and contribute to each other in complex ways. It is fairly obvious that, in most multiracial or multi-ethnic societies, class intersects with race and ethnicity, so that the most class-exploited groups tend to also have distinct racial or ethnic profiles. Race and class combine or interlock to oppress people in certain ways. This is an example of the kind of thing that the concept of intersectionality is about.

↓ Check Your Privilege!

You may have heard the expression 'check your privilege'. What does it mean? It is, quite simply, a suggestion or request for people to reflect on the ways in which their experience of the world, or perhaps of a specific kind of social situation, is shaped by different forms of social advantage or privilege. As such, it is also a suggestion or request to reflect on the fact that other people may have different, less privileged, or disadvantaged experiences of the world or situation, such that one's own experience cannot just be assumed to be the norm or how things are for everyone.

In a 1989 magazine piece entitled 'White Privilege: Unpacking the Invisible Knapsack', white American feminist scholar and activist Peggy McIntosh proposed the notion that white privilege is 'like an invisible weightless knapsack of special provisions, maps, passports, codebooks, visas, clothes, tools and blank checks'.

Privilege Checklist

Peggy McIntosh proposed a list of some of the ways in which privilege may manifest in daily life for a white woman like herself. For example:

- I can turn on the television or open to the front page of the paper and see people of my race widely and positively represented.
- When I was told about what is positive in our national heritage [in America] or in civilization, I was shown that people of my colour made it what it is.
- I am never asked to speak for all the people of my racial group.

Class

SARA R. FARRIS

Class is one of the most important dividing lines between people in our capitalist societies.

The concept of class is the elephant in the feminist room. It is always there, but it's not mentioned very often. In many ways, feminist movements from the very outset have been an attempt to overcome class divisions, namely, to unite women from different social backgrounds under the same roof. All women, after all, experience forms of violence and oppression – within and outside the home – which are specific to women as women, or to those who identify as women.

Yet, the ways in which women can and do respond to and react against violence and oppression differ greatly, depending upon their social location and class belonging. Think of how poor women find it harder to leave an abusive relationship because they cannot afford to live on their own financially, particularly when they have children. Or reflect on how difficult it can be for working-class women to participate in feminist meetings and collectives, given their long hours at work and/or the unaffordability of childcare.

These class differences have traversed the so-called three feminist waves. Even though the wave metaphor that is applied to the history of women's mobilisations is problematic – not least because it tends to be Westocentric and to blur the great heterogeneity of feminist movements – it is useful to succinctly capture the class tensions that characterised these movements through time.

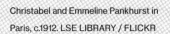

Christabel and Emmeline Pankhurst in Paris, c.1912. LSE LIBRARY / FLICKR

During the first wave, between the end of the nineteenth century and the first quarter of the twentieth century, the main fights of the growing women's movement were the right to vote and political equality. Indeed, in the West, like in many other regions of the world, women lacked political rights as they could neither elect their representatives in parliament through democratic elections nor run as candidates for political parties themselves. However, when British women, for instance, finally obtained their right to vote through the 1918 Representation of the People Act, property-less working-class women were excluded and remained disenfranchised until 1928. In many ways, this happened because many of the original suffragettes were middle-class homeowners who were not sensitive to the demands of working-class women.

The second wave, which coincides with the large mobilisation of women of the 1960s and 1970s, was mostly focused on reproductive and economic rights. Until the late 1960s and early 1970s, abortion was still illegal in the majority of Western countries and only became lawful (albeit with restrictions) after huge women's protests. Similarly, until the 1970s, the majority of (white) women in the West did not actively participate in waged labour outside the household and were excluded from many occupations or did not have the same working rights as men. It is only from the mid- to late 1970s that a growing number of women – thanks, once more, to the efforts and campaigns of feminists – began gaining economic independence through waged work. Here again, though, class distinctions heavily

Class Difference in the Suffragettes' Movement

The class tensions within the first-wave feminist movement, particularly in Britain, have been well documented. For instance, in *Pacifists, Patriots and the Vote* (Palgrave Macmillan, 2007), historian Jo Vellacott argues that the splits within the main suffragist organisations in the UK from 1915 onwards led to them being controlled by a small group of middle- and upper-class women based in London, with no representation of working-class women and the industrial North. Feminist historian Laura Schwartz more recently published a book – *Feminism and the Servant Problem* (CUP, 2019) – exploring the relationship and conflict between the pro-vote women's movement and the rising domestic workers' organisations, which represented the female servants who were often employed by the suffragettes themselves.

marked the ways in which women have enjoyed the fruits of these important battles – or were able to participate in these battles in the first place.

Concerning abortion, whilst in the UK the majority of women who seek abortion come from the poorest segments of society, in the US, working-class women are the ones who find it harder to access family planning, a situation that aggravates their economic marginalisation. Women's economic position in both cases is thus the primary reason why women do or do not exercise their 'free' choice to have an abortion (even as this choice is no longer mandated on the federal level in the US due to the Supreme Court's recent overturning of women's constitutional right to abortion). Concerning women's access to waged labour, whilst it has been a very important feminist achievement which enabled many women from different social backgrounds to gain economic independence, the type of job and the working conditions women have found are largely determined by and determine their class position and thus how the very hard-won economic independence can be enjoyed. For many working-class women, being employed in poorly paid sectors such as retail, care or primary education means that they have low wages, long hours and precarious contracts, thereby preventing them from having fulfilling independent lives.

The third wave is conventionally considered to have started in the 1990s and is characterised by at least two important developments. The first is the reworking of the concept of gender, after Judith Butler's landmark intervention (see: Sex/Gender p.10). The second is the fact that intersectionality has become – as feminist Kathy Davis put it – the new buzzword of feminism (see: Intersectionality p.50). Not only has it attracted attention from a countless number of scholars, but it has also become the keyword of contemporary feminist activism, and attempts to integrate an intersectional approach into national and international anti-discrimination law have become increasingly successful.

Intersectionality, or the special focus on the forms of oppression experienced by nonwhite, non-heterosexual, non-middle-class and non-abled bodies, was in many ways a reaction to what was perceived as the homogenising tendency of second-wave feminism, for which womanhood tended to coincide with the grievances and theorisations of white, middle-class women.

Whilst a concern with class has always been present within intersectionality, the framework has been criticised for turning class into one of the interlocking domains that is constantly enunciated but not really explored in any depth. One of the criticisms leveraged at intersectionality from a class perspective is that it conflates the workings of class with other categories, which operate according to different logics.

For instance, intersectionality's conflation of different categories such as race, gender and class obfuscates the fact that these categories adopt different political strategies. Whilst the political strategy that emerges from a focus on sexuality and gender can often be one of recognition within the realm of equal rights, that of class is a strategy of abolition. Indeed, the logic of class cannot be easily accommodated within the paradigm of political equality, which has been the dominant one within feminism.

Intersectionality and Class

Intersectionality theory (IT) has been criticised for treating all forms of oppression as equivalent categories, as well as for overlooking class. However, many feminist thinkers who have contributed to IT – either explicitly embracing and developing the concept or adopting an intersectional approach before the term had been coined – have paid sustained attention to class. These include Angela Davis, Patricia Hill Collins, bell hooks, Nira Yuval-Davis, Linda Martín Alcoff and others.

→ Political Equality

The language of rights and political equality is limited because it obscures how working-class women cannot enjoy full political equality.

For the feminists who underscore the key importance of class to the emancipatory project of women's self-determination, one of the problems with the paradigm of political equality that has dominated the various 'waves' of the feminist movement is that it is inadequate when addressing class divisions. Demands for equal rights indeed obfuscate the ways in which the paradigm of equality is predicated upon an abstract subject of rights who turns out to be white and middle-class.

The paradigm of universal political equality in the West conventionally stems from the Universal Declaration of the Rights of Man and the Citizen, one of the most significant outcomes of the 1789 French Revolution. From that declaration onwards, we have been accustomed to the idea that all human beings have natural, universal rights that should be upheld and respected. In the midst of the French Revolution, feminist thinker Olympe de Gouge unmasked the partiality of the claim to universality when she noted that the Universal Declaration of the Rights of Man and the Citizen mentioned only men, thereby leaving out half of the human population. Furthermore, during these same eventful years, it took Black slaves in the French colony of Haiti to show that the supposedly universal declaration of human rights excluded not only women but also many men: indeed, slaves in the colonies and property-less, working-class men certainly could not enjoy the same rights. From 1791 to 1804, Haitian slaves engaged in one of the most extraordinary anti-colonial revolts in history, which grew into the first successful revolution led by slaves and showed very concretely the hypocrisy of the paradigm of universal political equality.

This brief detour helps clarify a complicated but essential issue when it comes to understanding the differences between a political strategy focused on political equality and rights – which has been the predominant strategy of the feminist as well as other movements – and political strategy based on class.

Olympe de Gouge and the slaves in Haiti unmasked the fact that the horizon of political equality opened up by the French Revolution through the language of universal equal rights was a mirage for most, because it was based upon the needs and interests of white, middle- and upper-class men. Unsurprisingly, property-less men and all women continued to be excluded from the political franchise for more than a century. However, when women finally were able to vote, it was only wealthy women (as already noted) who were admitted to the club of the politically equal, thereby reproducing the exclusions that had already been enacted at the beginning of the movement for universal suffrage in the aftermath of the French Revolution. Furthermore, slavery continued to be the beating heart of colonial capitalist economies until the end of the nineteenth century. And, even when slavery was legally abolished, Black people in the US – the large majority of whom were poor and working-class – continued to be officially segregated and excluded from many services and spaces until the late 1960s.

For those who stress the importance of class for feminism, the language of rights and political equality is limited because it obscures the ways in which poor, working-class women (and working-class people more generally) cannot enjoy rights and political equality in their fullest sense. In the UK, for instance, most poor and working-class women are not eligible for legal aid, and thus find it harder to denounce domestic abuse and violence, or to defend themselves in court against wrongdoings of different sorts. Another example is that of migrant domestic workers in the UK, who have only a few months to flee an abusive employer and change jobs or risk violating the requirements of their visas and being deported. In all these cases, the claim to universal political equality, or to equal access to justice as women and human beings, is systematically denied or diminished for working-class women. This does not mean that the battle for political rights and universal equality is unimportant or not useful from a class perspective. On the contrary: the horizon of universal political equality has allowed many working-class women and marginalised subjects to gain recognition, and, as a result, the lives of many have improved. However, a class-based critique of political rights stresses that the framework of rights cannot fully address class inequalities because those inequalities are so rooted in our societies as to prevent access to political equality in the first place. For the class-based critique of political equality, true equality can only be achieved in a classless society.

But what is class? And how have feminists defined it?

In the social sciences, there are two main approaches to class: (1) the stratification/difference approach and (2) the antagonism approach. Those who endorse the first approach classify people into different groups, or 'classes', based upon people's income and status. These approaches understand class as a marker of difference and usually represent class society as a layered pyramid. The people at the bottom layer of the pyramid – the largest percentage in society – are those who earn the least and have a lower social status, whereas those at the top are the highest earners with the greatest social status.

The second approach was put forward by Karl Marx and maintains that the most important criterion to classify people into different classes is their relationship to three main forms of revenue: wages, profit and ground rent. People who live on wages – or the working class – are those who do not own the means of production, namely, the tools that allow them to work (be it their office space, or the computer they use at work, or the machinery they need to perform their jobs). Waged workers depend upon profit-makers, i.e. the second main class, who are the owners of the means of production. Unlike the stratification approach, the antagonism approach aims to describe classes not as unrelated, distinct groups but as social relations of interdependency and antagonism. The wage earners need the employers (profit-makers) in order to pay their bills and to subsist; but the employers need the wage earners to do the work that allows them to make their profit and stay at the top of the social hierarchy. The antagonism between the two classes derives from the fact that their members have contrasting interests, since both groups would be better off if each of them were not to maximise their earnings.

Even though the political strategy of a class perspective is abolition, feminists attentive to the logic of class inequalities have learned all too well that a classless society would not necessarily entail freedom and equality for all women.

Some feminists have contributed their reflections to the antagonism approach in particular and claimed that women are a class of their own, with men being the main antagonistic class.

In the 1970s, for instance, two very influential thinkers – Christine Delphy in France and Shulamith Firestone in the US – maintained that women are the subjugated class, or the underclass, who are oppressed by men as their domestic servants or as their sex slaves. The only way for women to free themselves, according to these thinkers, is to withdraw their domestic labour or sex. What is interesting here is that both Delphy's and Firestone's definitions of women as a class reject the concept of class in its more frequent economic meaning. In other words, both the stratification and the antagonism approach, in spite of their important differences, consider class as a category that describes the relation an individual has to wages and their access to economic resources.

Delphy's and Firestone's definitions tend to represent class as a category that describes the hierarchical relationship between men and women, with the latter being in a position of subordination and oppression. Their definitions are contentious, as they entail that there is more solidarity between people of the same sex/gender in spite of their contrasting economic interests – an idea which is often contradicted by the reality of class divisions described above.

Delphy's and Firestone's position that class is based on gender oppression highlights an important dimension of social class from a feminist perspective: whilst class is a social relation of interdependency and antagonism bringing together women and men who share their dependency on wages, class is also a relation of oppression which can pit people of the same class against one another. For instance, within the same working- or middle-class household, men can and do oppress women, particularly as the gender division of labour has for centuries

Other Feminist Approaches to Class

More recently, Marxist feminist thinkers have revived discussions about feminism and class:

- Cinzia Arruzza, for instance, argues that we need to understand the deployment of the strike as a strategic political tool in recent women's mobilisations as a feminist class struggle.
- Tithi Bhattacharya proposes that the framework of social reproduction – namely, the approach that focuses the caring work that women do within and outside their workplace – is essential for understanding feminist class struggles.

Suggested Resources

Skeggs, Beverley. 'Class'. In *Handbook of Marxism*, edited by Beverly Skeggs, Sara Farris, Alberto Toscano and Svenja Bromberg. Sage, 2021.

Davis, Kathy. 'Intersectionality as Buzzword: A Sociology of Science Perspective on What Makes a Feminist Theory Successful'. Feminist Theory 9, no. 1 (2008).

Vellacott, Jo. *Pacifists, Patriots and the Vote: The Erosion of Democratic Suffragism in Britain during the First World War*. Palgrave Macmillan, 2007.

segregated the latter into tasks that capitalist societies have largely devalued (i.e. caring, cooking, cleaning).

Even though the political strategy of a class perspective is abolition, feminists attentive to the logic of class inequalities have learned all too well that a classless society would not necessarily entail freedom and equality for all women. For instance, during the 1960s and 1970s, at the peak of the second-wave feminist movement, many of the women who joined the communist and socialist organisations advocating for the abolition of class society found that they were not treated as equal political allies or interlocutors. Instead, while men were the leaders and were given prominent roles within these organisations, women more often found themselves relegated to technical tasks, and their demands for gender emancipation were not taken seriously.

Does all this mean that class solidarity is inevitably a pipe dream or a mirage, like the idea of classless solidarity among women as women? Not exactly. What these experiences teach us is that class is a social relation inevitably entangled with other social relations, such as gender and race, for instance. Working-class people are also gendered and racialised subjects who embody and experience the wider contradictions and inequalities that come with these social relations.

Trans

CHIARA PELLEGRINI

Trans justice is a feminist issue.

Key Terms

Intersex

Intersex individuals are those whose sex is not deemed to fit typical definitions of maleness or femaleness. Intersex variations are very common, and they are characterised by some coexistence of what are supposedly separate male and female characteristics at the level of hormones, chromosomes or anatomy. Some trans individuals are intersex, and some intersex individuals are trans, but the two are not the same.

Heteronormativity

Heteronormativity is the institutional and collective privileging of heterosexuality, especially in those forms that characterise the lives of the people who have the most power. People who do not conform to those modes of heterosexual coupling, family life, child-rearing, gender roles or sexuality that are considered normal will be singled out as less normal and risk marginalisation, subordination and harm.

→ What We Mean by Trans

Trans is an umbrella term used to designate people whose gender is not the same as, or is not adequately described by, the gender they have been assigned at birth. Trans can be associated with identities like gender-diverse, gender-non-conforming, genderqueer, non-binary, transgender, transsexual and more. At the beginning of the twentieth century, terms like transsexual and transvestite were used to describe some of the individuals who might now call themselves trans. In the 1990s, the term transgender emerged as an alternative, together with its opposite, cisgender. Activists and academics like Sandy Stone (see Suggested Resources) sought to move away from words like 'transsexual' because these terms historically linked being trans to an illness that needed to be treated. Now, the concerns of trans communities and their allies have shifted beyond a focus on what trans is (who can be designated as trans, what causes someone to be trans) and towards how we can foster justice, safety and joy for trans and other marginalised subjects by challenging hetero-patriarchal, white supremacist and neoliberal forces.

Historically, trans aligns with Black feminisms, queer feminisms, disabled feminisms and others in asking the question 'Who does the term "women" implicitly exclude?' Despite views that see feminism and transness as incompatible (see: Trans and Feminism, p.76), trans and feminist activism, academic scholarship and culture have much in common and are often one and the same: they are dedicated to questioning and dismantling gendered hierarchies and patriarchal and heteronormative impositions that dictate which bodies, politics and social relations are the 'right' or 'normal' ones.

→ T and the Other Letters

In acronyms like LGBTQ+, trans is included alongside lesbian, gay, bisexual and queer (and others that follow the plus, such as intersex). Generally, these latter terms are seen as concerning sexuality (see: Sexuality p.20), whilst trans is seen as concerning gender identity (see: Sex/Gender p.10). Talking about someone's gender (who they are, how they present, what their relationship to the man/woman binary is, etc.) is not the same as talking about their sexuality (whom they have sex with, what kind of sex they have, what their relationship to heteronormativity is, etc.). However, they are not entirely separate either. Individually, one's gender and one's sexuality inform each other. Collectively, the kinds of justice and futures that LGBTQ+ communities and allies fight for are, more often than not, the same: ones in which heterosexual, binary and fixed identities (as well as whiteness and participation in capitalist processes) are no longer privileged or causing harm to those who do not conform to them.

Suggested Resources

Stone, Sandy. 'The Empire Strikes Back: A Posttranssexual Manifesto'. *Camera Obscura* 10, no. 2 (1992), https://sandystone.com/empire-strikes-back.html.

Gossett, Reina, Eric A. Stanley and Johanna Burton. *Trap Door: Trans Cultural Production and the Politics of Visibility.* MIT Press, 2017.

Malatino, Hil. *Trans Care*. University of Minnesota Press, 2020, https://manifold.umn.edu/projects/trans-care.

→ The Stakes

The very survival of trans individuals, as well as their access to healthcare, housing, education and social and political life, is at stake whenever we talk about gender. This is because discussions, policies, laws and social conventions involving 'men' and 'women' always imply a particular understanding of where trans and non-binary people stand in relation to these categories, resulting in inclusions and exclusions that impact their safety and rights. Gender-diverse people have always existed, and they face real risks; this is especially true of trans people who are not wealthy, white or legible through a clear gender binary, whose lives are under threat all over the world. A trans-inclusive feminism is the only feminism that adequately recognises these stakes.

→ Trans Narratives

Narratives are important: we understand gender through the stories we tell.

In the past few years, we've seen an increase in the visibility of trans stories. In 2014, an article in the American magazine *Time* announced a 'transgender tipping point': a new era in which the transparency of openly trans celebrities was declared as 'improving the lives of a long misunderstood minority'. The stories of prominent trans figures (mostly trans women) have been highly sought after by the media for decades and have often reached global audiences, from Christine Jorgensen's in the 1950s, to Caroline Cossey's in the 1980s, to Caitlin Jenner's in the 2010s. The way that these stories are reported is often sensationalist and aims to exoticise their protagonists, emphasising their difference from the majority of readers. If we have now reached the tipping point of trans visibility, it's important to ask: What exactly is visible, and what remains obscured?

As another key site for the production of trans stories, the trans memoir is a highly recognisable genre that comes with particular expectations. Traditionally, this kind of story traces the emergence of the narrator's identity against the gender they have been assigned at birth. As is particularly the case with twentieth-century memoirs, the story is structured as that of a person moving from one gender to the other. In this progress from A to B, there are some recurring tropes and motifs that readers have come to anticipate: an unhappy childhood, in which the protagonist is made to conform to gender norms that are alien to them; a period of testing out one's 'true' gender, often against the explicit prohibitions of parents and others; a moment of epiphany in which the trans person finally embraces their gender; and, then, specific steps to medically and legally transition, leading to a happy ending in which the protagonist's gender and body are aligned.

The popularity of this narrative has been instrumental in legitimising the lives of some trans individuals. However, as trans folks continually point out, this is not the whole story. The fact that this narrative is so pervasive is partly due to the expectation that this is the only possible trans story: this is what we think being trans is, and those who do not conform to this narrative are not as readily understood as trans. This can sometimes have material consequences: for instance, trans individuals can be denied the medical interventions or legal recognition that they need to be themselves on the basis that they are not recognisably trans.

Narratives that challenge this model in which the protagonist journeys from one gender to another are, by now, widely available, and they reveal what trans stories have been left out:

- Stories that are embedded in a community rather than about individuals pursuing an objective in isolation from others.

- Stories that are not legible according to Western understandings of gender, sex or social life.

- Stories that do not start or end with a specific binary gender, or with an ostensibly completed process of transition, but instead embody in-between-ness.

- Stories that take the emphasis away from transition, or even gender, showing that trans sits at an intersection with other aspects of identity, and that a trans author or character is more than their transness.

Trans authors write and publish not only personal autobiographical stories. Science fiction, fantasy, horror, literary fiction, poetry and experimental prose, and young adult literature are some of the genres in which trans characters, and new ways of viewing gender and the body, expand and enrich our understanding of what stories can do.

Try These Narratives!

Some trans novels in English that question conventions:

- River Solomon, *An Unkindness of Ghosts* (Akashic Books, 2017)

- Leslie Feinberg, *Stone Butch Blues* (Firebrand Books, 1993)

- Alison Rumfitt, *Tell Me I'm Worthless* (Cipher Press, 2021)

- Kai Cheng Thom, *Fierce Femmes and Notorious Liars* (Metonymy Press, 2016)

- Torrey Peters, *Detransition, Baby* (Profile, 2021)

- Akwaeke Emezi, *Freshwater* (Faber & Faber, 2018)

These little words describe something specific and elusive at the same time.

When speaking about people in the third person, we use pronouns that have certain gender associations. When we use a third-person pronoun for someone, we often make an assumption about their gender, and these assumptions are not always correct. But using the wrong pronoun for someone can have a dehumanising effect. Finding out and using a person's pronouns is an ethical gesture that shows respect and affirms their identity, just like using someone's correct name.

When we declare our pronouns (in emails, social media, virtual meetings, event name tags and so on), we indicate to others how to refer to us in the third person. When everyone does this, this can have the effect of normalising the signposting of one's pronouns, showing that it is not only trans or gender-non-conforming people who need to make their pronouns clear, as if their gender were more uncertain: no one's pronouns are more obvious than someone else's.

Someone's pronouns may be at odds with the assumptions we might make based on their appearance or name. This is especially the case when pronouns denote gender identities that are beyond the binary of male/female and the associated 'he' and 'she'. Some folks do not identify with the gender connotations of 'he' or 'she' and may therefore use gender-neutral pronouns for themselves.

In English, 'they/them' is the most common example, and has a long history of being used to refer in the singular to a person whose gender is unknown. There are also a number of neopronouns, such as 'ze' or 'hir', which may be new words, but the identities they refer to are not. It's also important to remember that third-person pronouns offer only a limited and finite number of ways to refer to a person: they are practical indications for mentioning someone in conversation, but they may not capture someone's gender in a full or precise manner.

It's normally pretty easy to find out someone's pronouns. Wikipedia pages, social media profiles or biographical blurbs will often refer to an individual in the third person in a way that we can usually assume to be endorsed by them (though at times such descriptions may not be up to date). Signposting our own pronouns, and encouraging others to do the same, can be a way to informally signal a commitment never to assume gender from conventional markers like names or appearance. However, this is different from demanding to know someone's pronouns. There are reasons why some individuals may not want to declare pronouns. Obligations to define, pinpoint and articulate our identities at all times should in fact be carefully questioned, as they characterise participation in a neoliberal society that demands that we put ourselves in the correct categories so that we can be better surveilled or marketed to.

Importantly, asking for pronouns should never be about making allies feel better because they can avoid mistakes, but about creating a safe and affirming space for everyone and recognising that others have authority in defining who they are.

How Does This Work in Practice?

https://www.mypronouns.org This website provides a practical guide on how to use gender-inclusive language in a variety of contexts and situations. Being attentive to how language can marginalise or harm others helps us put our feminism into practice.

→ Trans and Feminism

Trans feminists fight against patriarchal understandings of gender that harm everyone.

In the history of feminism, there have always been certain groups who think that trans women do not count as women, or who believe that allowing individuals to transition or recognising their gender goes against the aims of feminism. Though these groups by no means represent the majority of feminists, they currently hold a considerable amount of power and are very vocal in many countries. Trans-exclusionary feminists in effect threaten the rights and safety of trans people (especially trans women) based on their assumption that these rights are at odds with the rights and safety of cis women. They invalidate the identity of trans folks by invoking a notion of sex as innate, immutable and incompatible with its 'other' according to the male/female binary – a notion that the majority of feminists have instead always worked to undermine (see: Sex/Gender p.10).

This stance, at its best, fails to acknowledge that the patriarchal and heteronormative oppression faced by trans women is similar to the one faced by cis women, and, at its worst, perpetuates harm by wielding patriarchal and white supremacist tools (such as police and state intervention) against those who are most vulnerable. In countries like the US and the UK, trans-exclusionary feminist groups are, sometimes implicitly and sometimes explicitly, aligned with far-right (including nationalist and racist) values and organisations. This ideological affinity becomes clear when we reflect on how excluding trans women from female-only bathrooms, shelters, prisons, clinics, sport competitions or political groups is a way to enforce a rigid border between maleness and femaleness and cast trans individuals as dangerous others. The category of 'woman' becomes policed as a territory, into which entry can be gained only by those who have the right credentials. Trans-exclusionary feminists believe that, if trans women are included in this category, the meaning of 'woman' will be lost and the safety of cis women will be compromised. This way of viewing space through an 'us vs them' lens will likely ring a bell, as it is the same way in which nation and race are understood by anti-immigration and white supremacist politics: those who have less power and safety are cast as scary invaders who have come to threaten the identity of the insiders.

A trans-inclusive feminism recognises that trans individuals face sexism and are targeted by sexual violence resulting from the same patriarchal oppression that subordinates and threatens cis women. But the kind of problems that trans people face are not always shared by cis women. For instance, the former are often seen as not being real men or women, and face violence when others don't recognise their gender and view them as deceptive. Non-binary folks, instead, risk this violence precisely because they cannot or will not be understood as either men or women. Being gendered, facing gendered oppression and fighting for gendered rights will take different forms according not only to one's transness or cis-ness but also one's race, sexuality, nationality, class, religion and more. A trans-inclusive feminism can foster solidarity between those who suffer under the same system.

Suggested Resources

Sarah Clarke and Mallory Moore list some links between prominent gender critical feminists and far-right organisations here: https://transsafety.network/posts/gcs-and-the-right/.

Emi Koyama's 'Transfeminist Manifesto', an articulation of trans-inclusive feminism, can be found here: https://eminism.org.

Ruth Pearce Ruth, Sonja Erikainen and Ben Vincent's book *TERF Wars: An Introduction* (Sage, 2020) features global perspectives on how to achieve collaboration between trans and feminist movements.

Disability

CYNTHIA BAROUNIS

Categories of disability are socially constructed. They are also a source of pride for those marginalised by ableism.

Inspiration Porn

The media is flooded with feel-good stories about disabled people who overcome adversity or who receive spectacular forms of kindness or assistance from able-bodied saviours. We are far more likely to hear about Erik Weihenmayer, the blind man who climbed Mount Everest, or about a non-disabled student taking a student with Down's syndrome to the prom than we are to learn about airlines mishandling passengers' wheelchairs. This kind of media coverage is called 'inspiration porn' because it is designed for the emotional gratification of non-disabled viewers. Whilst inspiration porn may appear to be a positive representation of disability, it participates in the continued objectification of disabled bodies and distracts from the ableist barriers that disabled people contend with daily.

→ An Overlooked Minority

Like gender, disability is undeniably political. Access barriers and social stigma regularly affect the lives of people whose bodies and minds diverge from our culturally constructed idea of the norm. Indeed, there are many linkages we can make between the politics of disability and the politics of feminism and queerness. Yet, unlike other categories of marginalised identities (like race, gender and sexual orientation), disability is not always included in celebrations of diversity or in discussions about structural inequality. Even though disabled people compose one of the largest political minorities in countries like the United States, disability is commonly misrecognised as personal tragedy or individual misfortune. To understand why this is, we need to examine the medical model of disability which has been the dominant way cultures have understood disability, and we need to look at how it differs from the social model of disability.

→ The Medical Model

The medical model defines disability as an individual problem that can (and should) be solved through medical science. By reducing disability to a diagnosis, this model assumes that physical impairments are best addressed through medical treatments and rehabilitative technologies. When cure is not an option, the medical model expects disabled individuals to then triumph over their impairments through some combination of personal tenacity and medical or assistive technology. The medical model, for example, may expect a Deaf person to get cochlear implants or lip-read instead of using sign-language interpreters or captioners. This model is so deeply rooted in the way we talk about disability that it often masquerades as common sense. But behind this seemingly self-evident logic is the assumption that disability is something to be ashamed of or hidden. The underlying message is that disabled people can only participate in public life and social gatherings and have intimate relationships by 'overcoming' their disability and conforming to able-bodied standards as much as possible.

→ The Social Model

Disability scholars and activists have responded to these assumptions by developing the social model of disability. Rather than defining disability as an individual problem to be hidden or overcome, the social model defines disability as lack of fit between the body and its environment that leads to access barriers (see also: Bodies p.30). Such a 'misfit' might occur, for example, when a wheelchair user encounters a flight of stairs at the only entrance to a building. The wheelchair user's inability to enter the building is not the result of bodily deficiency but is the consequence of the fact that the building was constructed to accommodate only certain types of bodies. At its core, the social model is based on a belief that these access barriers have political significance. Promoting disability pride as an alternative to disability shame, the social model insists that disabled people should not have to modify their bodies or hide their disabilities in order to participate in public life.

Accessiblity

Accessibility means a lot more than ramps and elevators, even though these are two of the most commonly cited examples. Access may also include closed captioning on YouTube videos, extended time on exams, quiet rooms at conferences, trigger warnings, fragrance-free spaces, image descriptions of content that is posted on social media, a flexible absence policy in college classrooms – the list goes on. When trying to make a space or event accessible, it's important to consider how a range of bodies or minds might be implicitly included or excluded by the decisions that are made.

People-First Language

It is a common misconception that the most proper and respectful way to talk to or about a disabled person is to refer to them as a 'person with a disability' (instead of as a 'disabled person'). This is called people-first language or person-first language because it emphasises the person before the disability. Whilst person-first language is often well intentioned, it implies that a person's disability must be bracketed in order for us acknowledge their full humanity. Conversely, when we refer to someone as a 'disabled person', we are acknowledging that disability can be an important and valuable component of their identity. People-first language is generally rejected by disabled activists. At the same time, some disabled people embrace people-first language, and it is up to each individual disabled person to decide what language they would like to have used when describing them.

→ Beyond the Social Model

With its emphasis on disabling environments, the social model of disability works best when we apply it to more permanent and recognisable forms of disability, like mobility impairments and deafness. But this model may fall short when we expand our understanding of disability to include chronic pain and fatigue, psychiatric distress, asthma, diabetes and racial and class-based disparities in access to healthcare. Another limitation of the social model is that it doesn't have much to say about people who do not have impairments but who are positioned in an intimate relationship with disabled culture and community. This can include hearing children of Deaf adults or partners who provide care to their disabled partners. Alison Kafer's 'political-relational model' of disability makes room for this more expansive approach to disability. Departing from the social model's outright rejection of cure, the political-relational model acknowledges that some disabled people might pursue treatments or even cures on their own terms and not simply as a result of disability shame. The political-relational model also emphasises the crucial roles that relationships play in our understanding of disability, particularly those relationships that involve support and care. By broadening the disability umbrella, the political-relational approach helps us to think in more nuanced ways about how ableism connects to patriarchy, white supremacy and capitalism.

→ Madwomen and Disabled Divas

How does ableism help patriarchy pathologise women? What avenues exist for feminist/disabled coalition?

Sexism has long cast women as 'the weaker sex', but what role does ableism play in contributing to narratives of feminine frailty? Like disabled people, women are frequently mischaracterised as dependent, incomplete, helpless, incompetent and in need of rescue. Medical and philosophical texts dating back to antiquity have defined women as constitutionally weaker and more irrational than men. Historically, it is the male body that has set the standard for what a 'normal' and healthy body looks like, whilst the female body, by contrast, is often framed in pathologising terms (see: Bodies p.30). And yet, whilst women and disabled people might experience similar forms of oppression, it is also important not to conflate their experiences. Disabled women face unique challenges at the intersection of gender and disability, and those challenges have not always been reflected in traditional feminist organising.

 ↓ **Hysteria**

During the nineteenth century, doctors puzzled over the female reproductive system, treating it as a cause of mental distress and as a problem to solve. It was in this era that medical science invented the concept of hysteria, which originates from the Greek word for uterus and loosely translates to the phrase 'wandering womb'. When a woman behaved erratically or experienced depression, doctors did not acknowledge the environmental stressors that contributed to her mental distress. These stressors were, however, very often linked to a woman's lack of autonomy under patriarchy: the roles that left her confined within the home, the lack of a fulfilling career or outlet for her creativity and the pressures of motherhood and domesticity (see: Motherhood p.88 and Home p.110). Whilst depression

Jean-Martin Charcot demonstrating hysteria in a hypnotised patient at the Salpêtrière. Lithograph after P.A.A. Brouillet, 1887. WELLCOME COLLECTION

and anxiety may have been a reasonable response to these conditions, doctors tended to assume that hormones or a faulty uterus were to blame, and the treatments they prescribed only intensified women's domestic confinement.

Responding to this history, feminist thinkers of the 1970s sought to uncover the various ways patriarchy labelled women 'mad' when they stepped out of their assigned roles – or the way the stresses of sexism drove them to 'madness'. During this period, feminist literary scholars identified the figure of 'the madwoman in the attic' as a potent symbol of feminist rebellion. Whilst hysteria is no longer used as a diagnostic label, some feminists have argued that modern psychiatric categories, particularly those that are assigned disproportionately to women, like borderline personality disorder, are evidence of the way patriarchal medicine has adapted new methods for exerting control over women.

↓ The Limits of the Madwoman Trope

But what about those women who identify with their diagnoses and claim their psychiatric labels with pride? What are the consequences of interpreting psychiatric distress as merely a symptom of sexism? By transforming mental illness into a metaphor for feminist rebellion, these theories often overlooked the lived experience of women with psychiatric disabilities. More

'The madwoman in the attic' is a reference to the character of Bertha Mason in Charlotte Bronte's 1847 novel, *Jane Eyre*. Appearing towards the end of the novel, Bertha is revealed to be the wife of the main male character, Rochester, whom he has declared mad and locked away in his attic. She eventually dies after setting fire to the house. In their landmark 1979 book *The Madwoman in the Attic: The Woman Writer and the Nineteenth-Century Literary Imagination,* Sandra Gilbert and Susan Gubar argued that Bertha was labelled 'mad' only because she rebelled against her socially prescribed role as housewife. Her imprisonment in the attic therefore represents the many women whose voices have been silenced and whose power has been stolen by patriarchal medicine. Gilbert and Gubar use Bertha's character to showcase what they called the 'anxieties of authorship' that plagued creative and ambitious women in a culture that gave them only two possible roles: the docile 'angel in the house' or the unruly 'madwoman in the attic'. Notably, Bertha's character has a Creole heritage, making her mixed race.

recently, scholars in the emerging field of feminist psychiatric disability studies have highlighted how important it is to centre the voices and experiences of psychiatrically disabled women in feminist conversations about mental health.

Another limitation of the feminist preoccupation with hysteria is the fact that the diagnosis of hysteria was restricted to women of the middle or upper classes. The same doctors who deemed bourgeois women 'hysterical' used eugenic science to simultaneously argue that hysteria didn't affect women of colour and working-class women. Believing these women to be from 'less-evolved' races, they concluded that these women were sturdier and less delicate than their bourgeois counterparts, and that they were therefore better suited for manual labour and service occupations. In a more modern context, stereotypes of the strong Black woman and medical racism have made Black women and members of other racially marginalised communities less able to access psychiatric diagnoses and mental healthcare.

Bertha Mason, Jane Eyre; Illustrated by Edmund H. Garrett, 1897. BRITISH LIBRARY

Disabling Beauty Norms

The female body has been medicalised in other arenas as well. From the health hazards of nineteenth-century corsets to the growing epidemic of eating disorders, the pressure to conform to feminine roles can become literally disabling for certain women when taken to extremes. Meanwhile, cosmetic surgeries and other medical interventions that promise to 'fix' perceived bodily flaws are disproportionately marketed to women. Because these beauty standards promote a white Western feminine ideal, nonwhite women may confront additional pressures to use medicine as a way of whitening or Westernising their appearance (see: Race and Ethnicity p.42).

At the same time, women with visible physical disabilities often find themselves excluded from traditional feminine scripts related to beauty and desirability. Whilst non-disabled women are generally taught to understand themselves as sex objects for the male gaze and pressured into motherhood, disabled women frequently find themselves desexualised and are often expected to forgo motherhood altogether. Whilst there is some limited freedom to be found in escaping these traditional scripts, this exclusion has for the most part led to disabled women feeling a lack of physical autonomy and self-expression. Over the last two decades, however, disabled women have been slowly incorporated into the fashion industry. Models like Jillian Mercado and Aimee Mullins, and pop artists like Viktoria Modesta, have helped to reclaim and reshape the cultural image of disabled women by showing that disability, sexiness, and femininity can go hand in hand.

Suggested Resources

Garland-Thomson, Rosemarie. 'Integrating Disability, Transforming Feminist Theory'. NWSA Journal 14, no. 3 (Autumn 2002): 1–32.

Johnson, Merri Lisa. 'Neuroqueer Feminism: Turning with Tenderness toward Borderline Personality Disorder'. Signs 46, no. 3 (2021): 635–662.

Johnson, Merri Lisa. 'Label C/Rip'. Social Text Online, October 24, 2013, http://socialtextjournal.org/periscope_article/label-crip/.

Mollow, Anna. 'Mad Feminism'. Social Text Online, October 24, 2013, https://socialtextjournal.org/periscope_article/mad-feminism/.

Hedva, Johanna. 'Sick Woman Theory'. Mask Magazine, August 27, 2017.

Edgy and unapologetic, the term points towards a shared disability culture and a fierce opposition to able-bodied norms.

Compulsory Able-Bodiedness

In his 2006 book *Crip Theory*, Robert McRuer coined the term 'compulsory able-bodiedness' to describe the way that able-bodied norms, like gender norms, are something we are all pressured to perform repeatedly, regardless of our actual disability status. In order to manage our cultural anxiety over the fact that a truly 'able' body is a fantasy, we are asked to cover over that instability by continually affirming our commitment to able-bodiedness as an ideal. This term borrows from queer theory's concepts of 'compulsory heterosexuality' and 'gender performativity' (see Sex/Gender p.10).

The word crip is a variation on the ableist slur 'cripple'. Though derogatory in origin, crip has been subversively reclaimed by members of the disability community. Whilst the term disabled has been reclaimed in similar ways, it is also frequently used by those who subscribe to the medical model, making it less immediately clear whether the person using the term is an ally to the disability activist movement. The word crip erases some of that ambiguity. As an insider term, 'crip' can be found throughout the art, writing and performances that have emerged out of disability culture, from films like *Crip Camp and Vital Signs: Crip Culture Talks Back* to artist Sandie Yi's 'crip couture' and the #cripthevote hashtag.

In this respect, the use of the word 'crip' mirrors the use of the word 'queer' (see: Queer p.36). Both terms derive from insults that were initially used to demean and degrade a political minority, and both terms have been defiantly embraced in ways that transform their original meaning.

The similarities between 'crip' and 'queer' have led to some exciting alliances between disabled communities and lesbian, gay, bisexual and transgender communities, including the rise of the academic subfield of 'crip theory'.

Whilst there is no strict division between academic and activist uses of the word crip, scholars of crip theory have generally been most interested in the kind of work that crip can do to destabilise definitions of disability. Whilst disability is a term that we tend to apply only to people with physical and mental impairments, crip invites us to think in more expansive ways about who is negatively impacted by ableism, who participates in disability community and culture and how our social institutions are consistently pushing us to strive towards unreachable standards of physical and mental achievement, regardless of our disability status. As a result, crip theory tends to blur the lines between those who identify as disabled and those who identify as non-disabled.

Crip can therefore be understood not only as a noun (those who self-identify as crips) and an adjective ('crip culture') but also as a verb and an intellectual practice ('cripping'). To crip a concept or a text is to expose and deconstruct the very strategies through which that concept or text enshrines able-bodiedness as a cultural ideal. The practice of 'cripping' is often applied to phenomena that we may not immediately associate with disability.

One example of a concept that can be 'cripped' is the way we organise time. We don't always notice the way norms like a forty-hour work week, requirements around punctuality or even the way we romanticise spontaneous adventures are actually based on assumptions of able-bodiedness. These examples don't account for how chronic illness might affect someone's ability to work, how access barriers might add extra travel time or the necessity of advance planning to account for those barriers or to coordinate with caregivers and personal attendants. Other institutions or phenomena that have been 'cripped' include heterosexuality, capitalism, environmentalism, the university and, more recently, the COVID pandemic.

At the same time, the word crip is not embraced by all disabled people and its uses in both academic and activist contexts have generated some controversy. Some feel that the negative connotations of the term perpetuate disability stigma and approach it with discomfort. Furthermore, because the term creates space for non-disabled people to understand their lives in relationship to disability, some within the disability community have expressed discomfort and reservation about the way crip might be appropriated by non-disabled people or used in ways that divorce the term from its roots in disability culture and activism, including its incorporation into academic conversations. Finally, some feel that the word speaks exclusively to people whose disabilities are physical and visible, leaving out those who are neurodivergent or chronically ill. Whilst these critiques have sparked lively conversations, the term continues to be taken up by those within disability culture who identify with the word's transgressive connotations.

Krip

Some disabled activists and performers use the term 'krip' as an alternative to 'crip'. Leroy Moore, founder of the Krip Hop Nation project, explained that he used the krip spelling in order to differentiate his disabled performance group from the Crips, a Los Angeles–based street gang made up primarily of Black men. Whilst these disability and racial histories are distinct, some have also pointed to the ways these histories may intertwine, particularly as we consider the fact that disability can result from injuries related to gang violence. The term krip, then, is also a nod toward the intersections of disability, race and class.

Suggested Resources

Kafer, Alison. *Feminist, Queer, Crip.* (Indiana University Press, 2013).

McRuer, Robert. *Crip Theory: Cultural Signs of Queerness and Disability.* (New York University Press, 2006).

Kafai, Shayda. *Crip Kinship: The Disability Justice and Art Activism of Sins Invalid.* (Arsenal Pulp Press, 2021).

Wood, Caitlin, ed. *Criptiques.* (May Day, 2014).

Motherhood

SUZANNE LEONARD

Mothering is a contested concept in feminist thinking. Some find it a source of great power; for others, it is a profound oppression.

→ ## Is Motherhood a Choice or an Obligation?

Women have long been valued for their ability to mother, to the point that, at times, women's essential worth has been reduced to this capacity alone. Feminists the world over have argued against this singular valuation and chafed at the suggestion that mothering is the fullest possible expression of a woman's femininity. At the same time, feminism recognises that motherhood creates, nurtures and reinforces social bonds.

Implicit in the worldview which suggests that one is not a woman until one is a mother is a reliance on a rather conservative view of sexuality and sexual practice. This is to say, whilst sexual behaviour tends to be frowned upon for recreational purposes, when the goal is procreation, women are encouraged to give their bodies over to the act of heterosexual sex. A related conundrum is precisely the question of whose body should take precedence when a fetus is gestating. Many ethical, legal and moral quandaries arise when the needs, desires and practices of women are scrutinised based on the presumption that their lives are no longer fully their own.

Concerning the practice of mothering itself, whilst the act of raising a human is a noble calling, too often this labour is devalued economically, socially and legally. Motherhood might be revered rhetorically, but this language often lacks accompanying social policies and economic support structures. Specifically, many countries fail to pursue policies and community resources that ensure paid leave for parents, affordable child care, equitable health care, safe housing or quality education. Crucially and relatedly, one's experience of motherhood depends largely on structures of race, class, ethnicity and sexuality.

Feminists have come to challenge the white heterosexual mother ideal in order to better accommodate intersectional, queer, Indigenous and transnational identities (see: Intersectionality p.50; Queer p.36; and Race and Ethnicity p.42). Feminists also believe that biological reproduction is only one of a variety of ways to become a mother. An underlying ethos of the feminist movement is this: regardless of their identity category, people should be able to choose when, and if, they will become mothers, and if they do, parents and their children should be fully supported by the societies in which they live.

For these reasons and others, motherhood has been a vexed issue for feminism. We can trace this contradiction to the fact that there is no one definitive feminist answer to the following questions:

- Is motherhood a patriarchal institution that contributes to women's oppression?

- Is reproduction a unique capacity, which in turn affords mothers special skills and emotions?

- Does the fact that women are typically the ones to bear children automatically mean that they should be children's primary caretakers?

- To what extent is mothering an individual responsibility and to what extent is it a social and communal one?

- Who should pay and be paid for childcare?

- Does one have to identify as a woman to be a mother?

Precisely because these questions remain contentious, motherhood is an issue that has animated much feminist thought, discussion and theory.

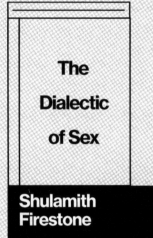

The

Dialectic

of Sex

Shulamith Firestone

The Dialectic of Sex: The Case for Feminist Revolution (1970)

Firestone located childbearing and the role of motherhood as the root cause of women's gender oppression. She wrote that 'pregnancy is barbaric', and imagined a utopian future in which biological reproduction would be replaced with ectogenesis, a process where embryos would gestate in artificial wombs in order to free women from 'the tyranny of reproduction'.

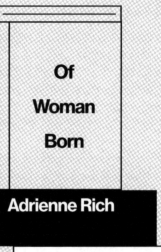

Of

Woman

Born

Adrienne Rich

Of Woman Born (1976)

Influenced by her experience raising three boys in the United States in the 1950s, Rich separated the act of mothering from the institution itself. It was the institution and the ideologies surrounding it, she argued, that relegated mothers to positions of inferiority. Her critique of the institution was withering: 'It has withheld over one-half the human species from the decisions affecting their lives; it exonerates men from fatherhood in any authentic sense; it creates the dangerous schism between private and public life; it calcifies human choices and potentialities. In the most fundamental and bewildering of contradictions, it has alienated women from our bodies by incarcerating us in them.'

Maternal Thinking

Sara Ruddick

Maternal Thinking: Towards a Politics of Peace (1989)

Looking at the practice of mothering rather than the institution, Ruddick considers 'the thinking that grows out of the work that mothers do'. Ruddick identified three primary components of maternal thinking: preservation (as in protecting), fostering growth and ensuring social acceptability. She saw all three as cognitive modes essential to creating healthy humans – and healthy societies – and proposed that they be harnessed in order to promote a nonviolent approach to conflict.

Black Feminist Thought

Patricia Hill Collins

Black Feminist Thought (1990) and 'Race, Class, and Feminist Theorizing about Motherhood' (1994)

Collins argued that feminist research on mothering had excluded race and class as conceptual categories. She identified the public/private divide (see: Family p.104 and Home p.110) as rooted in racialised understandings and reiterated that women of colour have long worked outside the home. Collins was particularly attentive to the realities of mothering in Black communities, and called for a decentring of the white, middleclass, stay-at-home mother ideal. Collins also coined the term 'motherwork' to more accurately convey the experience of mothering in nonwhite communities, and argued that 'survival, power, and identity' are its most important preoccupations.

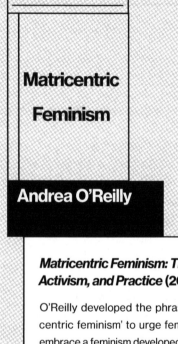

Matricentric Feminism

Andrea O'Reilly

Matricentric Feminism: Theory, Activism, and Practice (2016)

O'Reilly developed the phrase 'matricentric feminism' to urge feminists to embrace a feminism developed from the specific needs and concerns of mothers. Terming motherhood the 'unfinished business of feminism', O'Reilly asserts that many of the social, economic, political, cultural and psychological hurdles women face are specific to their roles as mothers.

The Maternal Imprint

Sarah Richardson

The Maternal Imprint: The Contested Science of Maternal-Fetal Effects (2021)

Richardson examines the burgeoning field of epigenetics, which contends that the intrauterine environment – including a woman's experiences, behaviours and physiology – can have life-altering effects on offspring development. These assumptions have staggering implications for gestating bodies (including the bodies of those who do not plan to mother), and often give cause for scrutinising the behaviours of people who are pregnant.

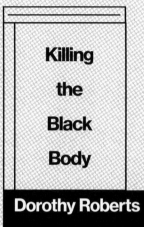

Killing the Black Body

Dorothy Roberts

***Killing the Black Body: Race, Reproduction, and the Meaning of Liberty* (1997)**

Beginning with American slavery, Roberts chronicles the war against Black reproduction. For centuries, measures have been put in place to contain, control and punish Black reproduction, including eugenics, forced sterilisation and welfare policies. Roberts argues that Black women's reproductive needs must be centralised in mainstream feminist and civil rights agendas.

The Mommy Myth

Susan Douglas and Meredith Michaels

***The Mommy Myth: The Idealization of Motherhood and How it Has Undermined All Women* (2004)**

Identifying what they call the 'new momism', Douglas and Michaels lament the resurgence of mythologies which situate motherhood as the most fulfilling life option for women. The zeitgeist set impossible standards for mothers to be judged and judge themselves by, and also reinforced capitalistic and competitive practices as the heuristics for judging 'good' mothering.

→ The Lived Realities of Mothering

The rhetorical switch from 'choice' to 'reproductive justice' changed the conversation about bodily autonomy, pregnancy, and social policy.

Othermothers

The tradition of othermothers is rooted in West Africa but widely practiced in the global diaspora. Othermothers provide care and socialisation for children who are not part of their immediate family units, and they help to rear children both inside and outside of the home, including in educational settings. Othermothers have been granted wider visibility within new family forms, including lesbian-headed families. However, othermothers have played valuable roles in their neighbourhoods and communities for centuries.

Originating out of the experiences of women marginalised by race, class and ability, reproductive justice grounds itself in the notion that abortion rights are not the only cause for which feminists interested in health policy must fight. Rather, reproductive justice advocates believe that all people must have access to contraception, comprehensive sex education, STI (sexually transmitted infection) prevention and assistance, adequate prenatal care, living wages and affordable housing. A direct and intentional expansion of the popular term 'pro-choice', reproductive justice looks holistically at the personal, legal and policy implications of reproductive health at all stages of a woman's life. Focusing on bodily autonomy and self-determination, proponents of reproductive justice assert that it is a human right to have a child and to parent in a healthy and safe environment. At the same time, they believe as strongly in the right not to have a child. Hence, they emphasise the need for abortion rights as forcefully as they do the notion that mothers and children must be afforded the resources they need to thrive.

ALFO MEDEIROS/PEXELS

Reproductive Justice Organisations

- ☐ SisterSong Women of Color Reproductive Justice Collective
- ☐ Women on Waves
- ☐ The Center for Reproductive Rights
- ☐ Birth Companions (in the UK)

Suggested Resources

Hondagneu-Sotelo, Pierrette. *Doméstica: Immigrant Workers Cleaning and Caring in the Shadows of Affluence.* (University of California Press, 2001).

Hochschild, Arlie, and Barbara Ehrenreich, eds. *Global Women: Nannies, Maids and Sex Workers in the New Economy.* (Metropolitan Books, 2003).

Salazar Parreñas, Rhacel. *Servants of Globalization: Women, Migration and Domestic Work.* 2nd ed. (Stanford University Press, 2015).

Oliveira, Gabrielle. *Motherhood across Borders: Immigrants and Their Children in Mexico and New York.* (New York University, 2018).

↓ The Motherhood Penalty

Referring specifically to the realms of work and economics, the motherhood penalty denotes the professional disadvantages that women face once they become mothers. At the most basic level, it is a wage penalty associated with the act of mothering, but it affects multiple aspects of a woman's career, such as her treatment whilst pregnant, ability to get hired, earnings, evaluations and promotions.

Women who raise children categorically fall behind men in salary and position, though this discrepancy is more pronounced for women of colour than it is for white women. Researchers contrast the motherhood penalty to the 'fatherhood bonus', meaning that men who become fathers tend to see wage and status advantages rather than disadvantages.

There are a number of factors which contribute to the motherhood penalty, including:

- the fact that women are more likely to take time away from the workforce or to reduce their work hours because of caregiving responsibilities;

- lacks in benefits such as paid parental leave, caregiving leave or flexible work schedules that make it easier to blend work and family life;

- outdated models that prioritise long, continuous, traditional work hours;

- women choosing lower-paying, family-friendly jobs in an effort to avoid punishing work schedules;

- the high cost of childcare, which pushes many women out of the workforce, particularly those who labour in low-wage industries;

- employers' assumption that women's caregiving commitments make them inappropriate candidates for demanding jobs.

Whilst one might assume that the motherhood penalty would not apply in countries that have paid family and medical leave, and in which childcare is subsidised by the government, this is in fact not the case. In reality, the motherhood penalty phenomenon is pervasive across all developed countries, although the severity of the penalties does differ by location. Researchers attempting to account for the persistence of the motherhood penalty speculate that the problem continues to come down to gender norms. Women remain disadvantaged by the view that they are more naturally suited to the role of parenthood than men, and hence should be the ones to take time away from work to fulfil those duties.

↓ Transnational Mothering

Transnational mothering occurs when mothers leave their children in their country of origin in order to work in a host country. The roots of these transitions are generally economic: women take positions as nannies, maids and household help in host countries and send money back to their homelands. This practice frequently involves what sociologist Arlie Hochschild has called 'emotional labor', insofar as domestic workers often care deeply for, and even love, the families for which they work. For many women, there are complicated emotional dynamics involved in nurturing children who are not biologically their own, whilst leaving the care of their own children to other family and community members, often in faraway places.

Suggested Resources

For more information on the reproductive justice movement in the United States, which is where the term originated, search for SisterSong Women of Color Reproductive Justice Collective.

For more on how to access medical abortion and information in countries and places where it is currently illegal, search for Women on Waves.

Care Work on Screen: Emotional Labour

The Managed Heart

'As traditionally more accomplished managers of feeling in private life, women more than men have put emotional labour on the market, and they know more about its personal costs.'

Arlie Hochschild. *The Managed Heart: Commercialization and Human Feeling.* Berkeley: University of California Press, 1983.

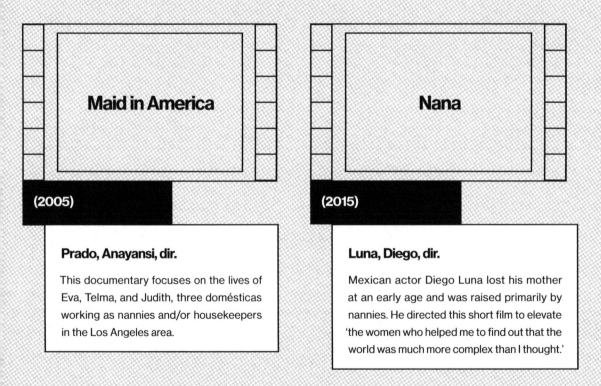

Maid in America

(2005)

Prado, Anayansi, dir.

This documentary focuses on the lives of Eva, Telma, and Judith, three domésticas working as nannies and/or housekeepers in the Los Angeles area.

Nana

(2015)

Luna, Diego, dir.

Mexican actor Diego Luna lost his mother at an early age and was raised primarily by nannies. He directed this short film to elevate 'the women who helped me to find out that the world was much more complex than I thought.'

In a 1983 study, sociologist Arlie Hochschild sought to understand the affective labouring conditions of flight attendants, with groundbreaking results. Borrowing from the Marxist insight that workers are alienated from the products they create, Hochschild coined the term 'emotional labour' to illustrate how interactions between flight attendants and their customers essentially divorce attendants from their own emotions. Workers must 'induce or suppress feeling in order to sustain the outward countenance that produces the proper state of mind in others,' feelings that are also quite difficult to turn off. Hochschild's insights have wide applicability, not just for retail industries, but for anyone charged with responsibility for another's emotions. Though now widely used as shorthand for affective, unpaid labour in the home, emotional labour has specific and important implications for those hired as in-house caretakers.

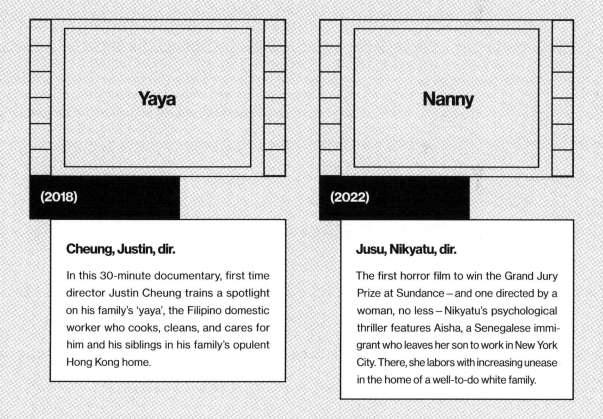

Yaya

(2018)

Cheung, Justin, dir.

In this 30-minute documentary, first time director Justin Cheung trains a spotlight on his family's 'yaya', the Filipino domestic worker who cooks, cleans, and cares for him and his siblings in his family's opulent Hong Kong home.

Nanny

(2022)

Jusu, Nikyatu, dir.

The first horror film to win the Grand Jury Prize at Sundance — and one directed by a woman, no less — Nikyatu's psychological thriller features Aisha, a Senegalese immigrant who leaves her son to work in New York City. There, she labors with increasing unease in the home of a well-to-do white family.

→ The Mamasphere: Motherhood in the Age of the Internet

Blogging, Postings, and Photos (so many photos...)

One of the many tenets of feminism has been the de-mystification of the motherhood ideal. Feminists have encouraged mothers to speak with candour about their physical, psychological and even spiritual experiences with pregnancy, labour and child-rearing. Yet, perhaps nothing has done more to give women a forum to publicise the actual reality of mothering than the internet. This digital area has been called the 'mamasphere', a term used to indicate a place where mothers talk about their views, experiences, practices and habits. Mothers also connect with each other in this space, commenting on each other's posts, sharing advice, and so on. Social media sites like Facebook, Twitter, Pinterest, Instagram and TikTok have also become go-to epicenters for the sharing of photos, practices and stories. Relatedly, collaborative online spaces like Mumsnet, Tumblr, and Reddit allow users to crowdsource questions and share experiences.

The mamasphere is typically thought to have originated with the practice of 'mommy blogging'. Researchers roughly date the height of the mommy blog era to 2005–2010, when bloggers wrote confessional, often humorous accounts of their daily realities, which were not necessarily attempts at profit making. Since then, a large number of individual blogs have spawned into larger content hubs, financed by businesses such as parenting magazines or product companies. Social media sites like Facebook, Twitter, Pinterest, Instagram and TikTok have also become go-to epicentres for the sharing of photos, practices and stories.

As the technologies have evolved, so has the purpose and system of rewards for digital practices. In their book *Mothering through Precarity: Women's Work and Digital Media* (Duke University Press, 2017), Julie A. Wilson and Emily Chivers Yochim argue that sites such as Facebook and Pinterest, as well as health and parenting websites, provide working- and middle-class American mothers with communities for material and emotional support. Some also become 'momprenuers' in an effort to sustain their families economically and emotionally. Wilson and Yochim argue that mothers navigate the brutalities of a highly neoliberal society, and also cultivate particular emotional realities – namely, 'happiness' – through their digital media practices.

By the early 2020s, the mamasphere had become heavily commercialised, populated by glossy content that is largely aspirational. Many content creators aspire to be 'momfluencers', meaning that they are sponsored by businesses for creating content that promotes a certain product, and some even become their own personal brands. Hence, a pronounced tension in the mamasphere is the contrast between transparency and commodified performance, although the lines between them are often quite blurry. Many momfluencers lean into the notion that they are imperfect wives and mothers, yet illustrate quite a different ethos with their cheerful comments and impeccable photos. Whilst some feminist researchers see the relational potential of spaces where mothers can connect, others are dismayed by what they see as the mamasphere's transition into a space compromised by capitalistic imperatives.

Motherhood in the Cinema of Pedro Almodóvar

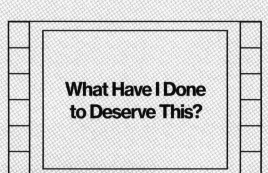

What Have I Done to Deserve This?

(1984)

An early film that helped to solidify Almodóvar's interest in desperate women and his penchant for finding outlandish solutions to their problems, *What Have I Done to Deserve This?* follows Gloria, a middle-aged housewife and cleaning woman who lives with her mother-in-law, two ungrateful sons and an abrasive husband. She eventually accidentally kills her husband with a ham bone.

All about My Mother

(1999)

Another of Almodóvar's suffering women, Manuela is a nurse who loses her son in a tragic accident and travels to Barcelona to connect with her son's other parent, now a trans woman named Lola. The film focuses on a community of women, many of whom are involved in the performing arts, who provide a kaleidoscopic picture of loss and trauma. The film nevertheless lovingly exalts the ways that identification between women – including a pregnant nun, a lesbian actress and a transgender woman – can lead to healing.

A queer filmmaker who grew up under Spanish dictator Francisco Franco's fascist government, Almodóvar has made a career out of portraying women – and especially mothers – with non-normative psychologies, behaviours and bodies. The director works primarily in the melodramatic mode, and his films tend to feature extreme circumstances and plotlines, images and colour that pop, twists of fate and a heightened attention to emotion. Motherhood is by far his favourite theme, and his oeuvre speaks to the need to examine mothers, and the act of mothering, with sympathy, humour and compassion. He is also unabashedly sex-positive and trans-positive, attitudes that are easily discernible in his films about mothers. Whilst Almodóvar has directed over twenty films to date, the following examples typify his contention that suffering and liberation must be examined conterminously.

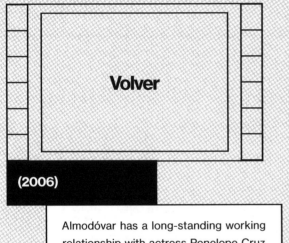

Volver

(2006)

Almodóvar has a long-standing working relationship with actress Penelope Cruz, who also appears in *All about My Mother* and *Parallel Mothers*. In this film, Cruz plays Raimunda, who rescues her daughter from an attempted rape by her stepfather (Raimunda's husband) by killing him with a knife. In keeping with Almodóvar's fascination with the bonds between women, the film focuses on Raimunda and her daughter, her aunt, her sister and finally her dead mother, who returns and may or may not be a ghost.

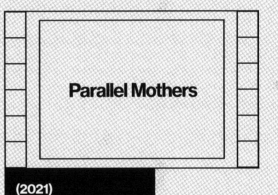

Parallel Mothers

(2021)

Parallel Mothers features Cruz as Janice, a woman in her forties who is happily preparing to give birth and raise her child as a single mother. In the hospital, she meets Ana, who is also single but in her twenties, resentful of her impending responsibilities and assisted only by her self-absorbed mother. Though the two women initially go their separate ways, their lives remain entwined thanks to a number of melodramatic plot twists, including mix-ups, last-minute reversals of fortune and mistaken identities.

Family

SUZANNE LEONARD

How can so many rights, privileges, and images and ideals rest on one single notion?

According to the most basic definitions, a family is a group of two or more persons related by birth, marriage or adoption. Despite the neutrality of this language, in the twentieth and twenty-first centuries, the term has conjured up an image that is probably best exemplified by the mid-twentieth-century American television show *Leave It to Beaver*: families consist of a mother, father and two or more biological children who live together. More pointedly, everyone is white, heterosexual and middle-class. Whilst it's clear that this picture is hugely problematic for all that it leaves out, the term 'family' has nevertheless been saddled by this expectation in many Western nations.

Feminists have sought en masse to challenge this assumption: many a feminist tract is organised around the idea of rescripting, rethinking or redefining the family. These interventions have upended every aspect of the quintessential family ideal. Feminists remind us that single parents have families, couples without children are families and same-sex couples with or without children are families. For many, 'chosen' families (which aren't related by birth, marriage or adoption, and don't necessarily live together) are the most valuable of all intimate ties.

The Family is Not the Private Sphere, and it *is* Political

Perhaps one of the most nostalgic mindsets that remains stubbornly in circulation is the idea that the family should serve as 'a haven in a heartless world'. In fact, such notions are heavily gendered and classed. In this rendering, domestic life is governed by 'feminine' norms of caring, compassion and sympathy, which are typically demonstrated by women and especially mothers. These invocations also assume the existence of safe, healthy spaces in which the basic necessities of life are met without struggle. The home is considered the training ground for good values, which are then passed on to children. On the other hand, the public sphere, which is associated with men, is opportunistic and capitalistic, driven by competition and ambition.

For feminists, these supposed divisions – typically called 'the public versus the private' – instantiate gender inequality, and also obscure the realities of family lifesee: Home p.110). For one, they rely on a monolithic, heteronormative ideal which assumes that families are created by a man and a woman. One of the many deceptions promulgated by this schema is that different emotions, attitudes and aspirations are exhibited by different genders, and simply being a husband or a wife, or a mother or a father, confers these attributes. They likewise encourage the assumption that women do not labour outside the home, that labour performed inside the home does not count as such and that men are not responsible for creating the home's emotional aura. These understandings of family leave little space to conceive of the home itself as a site of strife or even violence, or a place that mirrors the same power differentials as one finds in the public sphere.

Moreover, identities and roles associated with the family, such as being a husband or a wife, are titles that necessitate legal sanction. Enslaved people in the United States, for example, could not get married or have marriages legally recognised.

Legal recognition

It remains against the law in many places to marry more than one person, and gay marriage is illegal in many nations. Moreover, to be legally recognised as a spouse or parent confers a host of privileges: for instance, only people who are designated immediate family members are entitled to hospital visitation rights, child custody provisions, life and health insurance, retirement benefits and tax breaks. The notion that the family as a social grouping carries no ideological or political advantages is, in short, a convenient fiction.

→ Family Planning

It's about much more than birth control.

The term 'family planning' is generally used as a euphemism for birth control. In other words, whilst the term itself refers to the ability of individuals and couples to have their desired number of children – to time their births – it is commonly understood as employing precautionary measures, generally in the form of hormones or physical barriers, to avoid unwanted pregnancies. Whilst today there are many forms of contraception, the advent of the birth control pill was especially crucial in affording women the right to make these decisions, and in ways that did not depend solely on the involvement or consent of a partner. Yet, in the early years of its introduction, the birth control pill was only available to married women. However, this did begin to change in many Western nations in the 1960s.

The term 'family planning' also belies the long history of denying women the right to manage their sexual and reproductive health. Thus, it is crucial to recognise how difficult it remains for many women to access safe and reliable conception: many religions continue to frown on the practice, and some outright forbid it. Contraception is also unequally available throughout the world and can be particularly difficult for women from low-income countries to obtain. Finally, abortion, where a woman seeks to terminate a pregnancy, is a controversial practice that is outright outlawed in many nations. Feminists are generally in favour of abortion rights and have encouraged a redefining of the abortion debate away from the monikers 'pro-life' and 'pro-choice', preferring instead the terms 'anti-choice' and 'pro-choice'. They also situate abortion in a range of practices and attitudes referred to as 'reproductive justice', which refers to the human right to maintain personal bodily autonomy, have children or not have children and parent the children one has in safe and sustainable communities (see: Motherhood p.88).

↓ Alternatives and Assistance in Making Generations: Key Terms

Whilst biological reproduction remains the most widely used practice by which to have children, other options have made it possible for people to create families in other ways. These options have been particularly valuable for couples who have fertility challenges, single people, and the LGBTQIA+ community at large. These alternatives typically cost money, which is another way in which the family system cannot be separated from the public sphere. Legal and ethical issues surrounding these options are also of concern to feminists interested in how power differentials underpin all reproductive practices.

Adoption

The social, emotional and legal process in which children who will not be raised by their birth parents become members of another family. Adoptions confer a permanent change in status, so that the adoptive parent assumes all legal rights and responsibilities for the child.

Assisted Reproduction

An umbrella term for the multitude of options for having children with the help of medical professionals. More precisely, it involves the handling of eggs, sperm or both. The term covers artificial insemination, intrauterine insemination, in vitro fertilisation and ovarian stimulation.

Cross-Border Reproductive Care

The phenomenon of people crossing international borders to access reproductive technologies. One of the fastest-growing categories of cross-border reproductive care is international surrogacy.

Surrogacy

An arrangement where a gestational carrier bears a child for another person or couple. The surrogate may or may not use their own eggs, and monetary compensation may or may not be involved. In some countries, surrogacy is legal only if money does not exchange hands. (See: Health and Medicine p.132 and Timeline: Reproductive Medicine p.138.)

Childhood innocence: an origin story

Childless vs. Childfree by Choice

Since the early 2000s, there has been a telling change in the terminology surrounding women without children. Women's social value has long been tied to their images as nurturers and mothers, and so it was commonly assumed that women who could not or did not reproduce were emotionally and psychologically disadvantaged, hence the term 'childless' (see: Motherhood p.88). Of course, the condition of being without children has myriad root causes, and it can be volitional or not. For instance, the accessibility of parenthood is impacted by poverty, illness, infertility, poor nutrition or low marriage rates caused by wars. A new conceptualisation of 'childfree by choice' has, however, significantly reframed this cultural understanding to afford the condition a more positive valence. The language change is meant to signal that for many women, not having children is a preferred option to having them, and therefore such women do not consider themselves at a disadvantage.

During the Enlightenment period (typically dated from 1685 to 1815), the idea of the 'child' first took hold. Prior to this time, children were considered miniature adults rather than a category subject to special provisions and training. In 1762, French political philosopher Jean-Jacques Rousseau published *Emile*, a tract that is widely understood as introducing the now-accepted idea that children are inherently innocent beings who need education to prevent them from being corrupted by adult society. It is important to note, however, that childhood innocence as a concept was created in relation to white children specifically; nonwhite children did not, and do not, necessarily enjoy this privilege. A number of assumptions followed from this fundamental paradigm shift: for one, it was no longer acceptable to position children as labourers or wage earners; instead, their status shifted to that of economic dependents. Child labour laws followed. Education, both by formalised systems, and also by parents and caregivers, began to acquire value as an unquestioned social good. Children were understood as both vulnerable and immature, and hence in need of protection. (Many a moral panic has ensued when adults are pegged as corrupting influences.) Finally, entire industries have arisen to support the physical and psychological advancement of children, all premised on the understanding that this is a unique developmental period.

ALLAN MAS/PEXELS

↓ | Unmaking Families: Focus on Poverty

Whilst feminists have historically been very concerned with the conditions of people living within family structures, various forms of social inequality are often the root causes of what we can call 'unmaking families'. The list below is not exhaustive but is meant to illustrate that ways that families are separated or destroyed, and the role that power differentials play in this process. Many of these problems are impacted and exacerbated by class divides, and specifically by the role that poverty plays in determining family outcomes, all of which are feminist concerns.

The following are examples of families being unmade:

- ✚ children who are removed from 'unfit parents';

- ✚ families who are separated when trying to cross national borders;

- ✚ family members who are incarcerated;

- ✚ family members who are disappeared by their governments;

- ✚ family members who leave their biological families in one place in order to seek work in another;

- ✚ family members who are separated as a result of climate disaster;

- ✚ families that are torn apart by war or political conflict.

Gendering Children: Gender Essentialism verses Social Constructionism

The idea that boys and girls are fundamentally different beings due to their biology is called 'gender essentialism' (see: Sex/Gender p.10). Feminists generally resist these tendencies, preferring instead to think of gender as a social construction in which culture and society play a significant role (see: Race and Ethnicity p.42). Feminists also point to the fact that these supposed essential differences are used to justify different – and hence unequal – treatment between boys and girls and men and women.

Despite feminist resistance to the practice, children tend to be gendered from birth, in the sense that they are played with, spoken to and dressed differently based on their assigned sex. It is also common for certain activities, attributes and skills to be encouraged in one group but not the other. Attention has been paid recently to the question of how children may resist specific gender attributions, particularly when they feel at odds with the sex they were assigned at birth. Some children do not associate with either gender and are considered non-binary (see: Sex/Gender p.10 and Trans p.70).

Home

YOLANDE STRENGERS

Household labour remains persistently gendered, despite changes and shocks.

In Popular Culture

Feminists and gender scholars have pointed out the unequal division of labour in the home for generations. Popular culture, particularly 20th- and 21st-century US sitcoms and films, have idealised the heterosexual nuclear family on screen, and normalised the role of the highly competent and loving housewife, reinforcing these unrealistic gendered expectations (see: Family p.104).

→ Gender and the Home

The home has always been a deeply gendered space, with traditional gender roles still informing how housework, emotional labour, caring responsibilities and leisure activities are organised and carried out. Whilst there is considerable diversity across cultures, countries and households, in general women are still responsible for the majority of unpaid (and paid) caring and household tasks. This includes household administration and social management, housework such as cleaning, cooking and shopping for provisions, and parenting and caring for other household members such as children and ageing parents. Women also typically take on the role of household managers, which increases their mental load and can result in additional stress and burnout.

In reality, marriage strategically benefits men more than women in heterosexual coupled partnerships by increasing the workload for women whilst simultaneously decreasing it for men. Experts have called out the systematic barriers and social stereotypes that prevent men from undertaking more unpaid labour at home, such as flexible work options, paid parental leave and an enduring social expectation that childrearing is women's work. These gender imbalances in household labour have also been linked to the enduring gender pay gap, the lack of women in senior leadership positions and ongoing domestic violence.

→ Beyond the Nuclear Family

Heterosexual couples and families are not the only type of household configuration. In the US, 1.5 percent of households are in same-sex partnerships. Households are increasingly ageing at home, rather than moving into institutionalised care, which often involves reliance on unpaid care from a family member, most likely a daughter or a daughter-in-law. Single-person households are rising faster than families in some parts of the world, like the UK and Australia, with older women most likely to live alone. Conversely, overcrowded housing is rising in some countries and vulnerable communities, and can be a precursor to homelessness. Older women are particularly vulnerable to homelessness in affluent nations like Australia, and women are also disproportionately represented in the people who become homeless by fleeing domestic violence situations.

→ Pandemic: Progress or Problem?

The COVID-19 pandemic and associated lockdowns in many parts of the world have increased flexible working options for many, resulting in more people working from home. This has enabled greater flexibility for people juggling parenting, housework and paid working opportunities, and in some countries resulted in fathers in heterosexual couples with children increasing their contribution to domestic housework and caring labour, though not as much as mothers. Experts warn, however, that the fallout of the pandemic is likely to further exacerbate gender inequality. For instance, Australian and US scholars have found that the pandemic further entrenched women's (and particularly mothers') roles as the primary carers and unpaid labourers in the home, whilst simultaneously increasing their economic vulnerability. This has left them at risk of poor health, anxiety and stress.

Suggested Resources

Carson, Andrea, Leah Ruppanner and Shaun Ratcliff. 'Worsening of Australian Women's Experiences under COVID-19: A Crisis for Victoria's Future'. 2020. https://arts.unimelb.edu.au/the-policy-lab/projects/projects/worsening.

Ruppanner, Leah, Xiao Tan, William Scarborough, Liana Christin Landivar and Caitlyn Collins. 'Shifting Inequalities? Parents' Sleep, Anxiety, and Calm during the COVID-19 Pandemic in Australia and the United States'. Men and Masculinities 24, no. 1 (2021): 181–188.

Ruppanner, Leah, Xiao Tan, Andrea Carson and Shaun Ratcliff. 'Emotional and Financial Health during COVID-19: The Role of Housework, Employment and Childcare in Australia and the United States'. Gender, Work and Organisation 28 (2021): 1937–1955.

→ The Most Dangerous Place to Be?

New technologies are changing the techniques for domestic abuse and generating more housework.

According to the United Nations Office on Drugs and Crime, the home is the most likely place for a woman to be killed. That's because women are most likely to be murdered by their intimate partner or a family member (whereas men are more likely to be murdered by strangers). In 2017, over 50,000 women were killed by those closest to them – 137 women across the world every day. Whilst femicide is the most extreme form of violence towards women, it exists on a spectrum, with many other forms of domestic abuse (verbal, emotional and physical) and sexual violence also commonly occurring inside the home.

Indeed, coercive control – a form of domestic abuse that involves acts of assault, threats, humiliation, intimidation and control – often takes place within the home, with men the most common perpetrators. It can involve behaviours such as monitoring a partner's movements, not allowing them to leave the home or have relationships with other people, controlling their finances and communications or engaging in digital domestic abuse.

The criminalisation process for rape in marriage began in the 1970s in most countries. Marital rape became a crime in all fifty US states only in 1993 – and prosecution is still fraught. Spousal rape is still legal in at least ten countries, with consent implicit in the marriage contract. Spousal rape most commonly occurs in the home.

↓ Digital Domestic Abuse

Digital technologies are increasingly being enrolled in domestic abuse, including behaviours such as stalking, surveillance, harassment and control. This commonly takes place through smartphones, on which tracking apps can be installed (non-consensually), or which can facilitate techniques that enable such abuse. Emerging research is also exploring how smart-home technologies and the internet of things can facilitate domestic abuse – by locking people into or out of their house (via a smart lock), or by intimidating and gaslighting partners through techniques such as turning lights and other remotely controlled appliances on and off.

↓ Digital Housekeeping

Peter Tolmie and colleagues originally coined the term 'digital housekeeping' in reference to the networked home, to highlight the efforts involved in making the networked home work.

The term has since been taken up by other technology and feminist scholars to explore the gendered ways in which digital housekeeping occurs in households. Men are more likely to perform digital housekeeping in smart or automated homes, taking on the tasks of researching, purchasing, setting up, maintaining, replacing, tidying, updating and integrating these technologies into the home. Some scholars warn that an increase in digital housekeeping sits somewhere between a hobby and essential housework, and can take the digital housekeeper away from more traditional housework and caring responsibilities. In heterosexual homes, this can further entrench gendered divisions of labour.

Suggested Resources

Kennedy, Jenny, Bjorn Nansen, Michael Arnold, Rowan Wilken and Martin Gibbs. 'Digital Housekeepers and Domestic Expertise in the Networked Home'. *Convergence* 21, no. 4 (2015): 408–422.

Strengers, Yolande, and Larissa Nicholls. 'Aesthetic Pleasures and Gendered Tech-Work in the 21st-Century Smart Home'. *Media International Australia* 166, no. 1 (2017): 70–80.

Tanczer, Leonie, Ine Steenmans, Miles Elsden, Jason Blackstock and Madeline Carr. 'Emerging Risks in the IoT Ecosystem: Who's Afraid of the Big Bad Smart Fridge?' In *Living in the Internet of Things: Cybersecurity of the IoT* – 2018, https://ieeexplore.ieee.org/document/8379720.

Tolmie, Peter, Andy Crabtree, Tom Rodden, Chris Greenhalgh and Steve Benford. 'Making the Home Network at Home: Digital Housekeeping'. In *Proceedings of the Tenth European Conference on Computer Supported Cooperative Work* (2007): 331–350.

Primetime: Perfect Postwar American Housewives

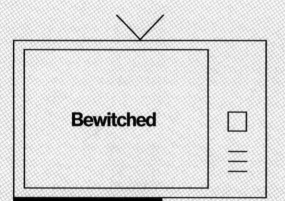

Bewitched

(1964–1972)

This American fantasy sitcom series featured a beautiful witch named Samantha, who marries an ordinary suburban man and vows to lead the life of a 'normal' housewife (as her husband wishes). However, Samantha's magical family disapproves of the union and frequently interferes in their lives. The show has been critiqued and celebrated for both reinforcing and subverting cultural stereotypes regarding gender roles and interracial marriage.

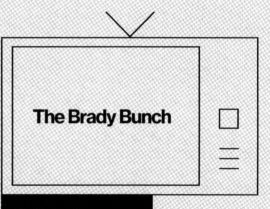

The Brady Bunch

(1969–1974)

An American sitcom series revolving around the lives of a large blended family with six children. Whilst husband Mike Brady is a widower with three boys, his wife Carol Brady's previous marital status (divorced or widowed) is never directly revealed. Carol is an ideal and stereotypical stay-at-home mother (supported by Mike's housekeeper, who joins the blended family) and also takes on paid work in the sequels as a real estate agent.

Sitcom wives have set an unrealistic benchmark and stereotype for women and families. The caring, loving and competent housewife (or the shocking opposite to this), has been a longstanding trope in twentieth- and twenty-first-century US sitcoms and films. This stereotypical woman (and her equally stereotypical husband) has reinforced gendered expectations for marriage and relationships for decades.

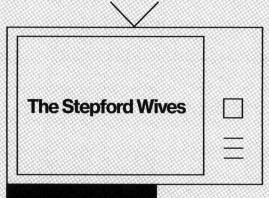

The Stepford Wives

(1972 and 2004)

Originally a satirical novel written by Ira Levin, *The Stepford Wives* has been made into two films featuring a suburban men's club which is secretly transforming their modern, assertive and independent wives into submissive and adoring housewives who dote on their every need and desire.

Married... with Children

(1987–1997)

This live-action sitcom follows the lives of husband Al Bundy, a disgruntled women's shoe salesman who constantly attempts to relive his youth as a successful high school football player; his lazy and shopping-addicted wife, Peggy; and their two children – Kelly (portrayed as a dumb blonde) and Budrick aka 'Bud' (a smart alec who is preoccupied with sex).

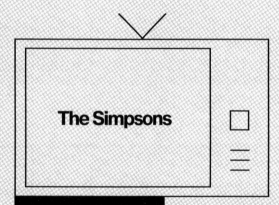

The Simpsons

(1989–ongoing)

The Simpsons is an adult animated sitcom and satirical depiction of American life, which features a dysfunctional family helmed by the continually incompetent yet well-meaning husband and father, Homer, who is supported by his loving and wise housewife, Marge.

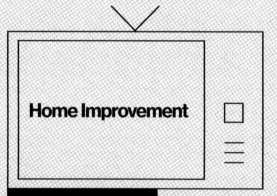

Home Improvement

(1991–1999)

An American television sitcom featuring the lives of the Taylor family which casts the main characters using stereotypically gendered tropes. Tim (the husband) loves power tools, cars and sports. Jill (Tim's housewife) provides emotional intelligence and support for her husband. In later seasons, she returns to college to study psychology.

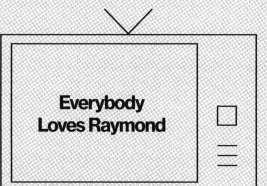

Everybody Loves Raymond

(1996–2005)

This sitcom television series follows the lives of a suburban Italian-American family who face continual interference into their lives from Raymond's family. Debra, Raymond's wife, takes on the majority of housework and parenting, and is continually frustrated by her husband's avoidance and incompetence with emotional labour, housekeeping and parenting responsibilities.

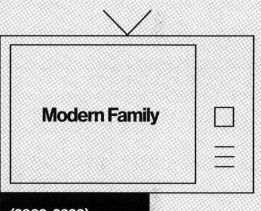

Modern Family

(2009–2020)

This mocumentary-style sitcom follows the lives of three different types of families (nuclear, blended and same-sex). Despite attempting to represent progress and differentiation in 'modern' families, the show was criticised during earlier seasons for casting women only as stay-at-home mums whilst the husbands have successful careers.

Key Feminist Thinkers on Housewives and Household Labour

The Feminine Mystique

Betty Friedan

The Feminine Mystique (1963)

Betty Friedan was a leading American feminist writer and activist who is most famous for her 1963 book, *The Feminine Mystique*. The book critiqued the roles of women in industrial societies, especially the full-time homemaker role, which Friedan found stifling. It was also credited as sparking the second wave of American feminism in the twentieth century. See especially her chapter 'Housewifery Expands to Fill the Time Available'.

Wifework

Susan Maushart

Wifework: What Marriage Really Means for Women (2001)

American author, journalist and feminist Susan Maushart wrote her landmark book *Wifework: What Marriage Really Means for Women* in 2001. The book mounts a scathing attack on the institution of marriage and how it disadvantages heterosexual women's lives and careers, leaving many unhappy. Key to Maushart's argument is the additional household labour women do in marriage.

The Wife Drought

Annabel Crabb

The Wife Drought (2015)

In 2015, Australian political journalist Annabel Crabb wrote *The Wife Drought* to call out the decline in housewives, whose traditional (full-time) job was to take care of the house and those who occupy it. Crabb calls attention to the drought afflicting households in general and women in particular, referring to the absence of a person within the home who can perform the traditional roles of the housewife.

→ Smart Homes for Whom?

Men are more likely to be interested in, and engaged with, smart home devices.

Smart-home technologies – featuring automated and remotely controlled lights and appliances, light 'scenes' and 'moods', integrated audiovisual and cinematic experiences, automated heating and cooling, energy management, security systems with real-time alerts and video monitoring and control centres or hubs to enable system integration – are becoming increasingly popular. The most enthusiastic take-up has been for off-the-shelf devices that users can easily set up themselves to plug and play. However, integrated and automated systems – with smart-phone, tablet, wall-operated and/or voice-integrated control stations – are also becoming more popular.

For many decades now, the vision of a smart home that takes care of itself and its occupants (including doing all the house-work) has been a utopian ideal that's 'just around the corner'. Westinghouse's 1930s 'Home of Tomorrow', for example, featured an astonishing number of appliances (even by today's standards) which were designed to ensure the occupants never needed to lift a finger. However, history demonstrates that these visions rarely deliver what they promise, and often raise lifestyle expectations in ways that ultimately increase domestic labour.

Whilst historically many household appliances have been marketed towards women, promising to free them of domestic drudgery, the smart home is mostly marketed towards men's leisure, positioning their technical competency as a masculine contribution to housework, care and parenting. Research shows that men are more likely to be interested in, instigate and lead smart-home setups in heterosexual relationships. Unfortunately, however, the hype rarely matches the reality, with smart-home setups generating new conveniences and comforts whilst simultaneously generating new labours in the home. Gender imbalances in who is interested in, and involved in setting up, smart-home devices have also been linked to these technologies' increasing role in digital domestic abuse.

Smart-Home Technologies

Ruth Schwartz Cowan's classic work of women's history on the industrial revolution of the home, *More Work for Mother* (1985), showed how labour-saving appliances like washing machines, irons and vacuum cleaners resulted in 'more work for mother', even though they promised to free up women's time from house-work. While they did increase time efficiencies, Cowan argues that these domestic technologies also raised standards for cleanliness, ultimately requiring more work from women to achieve heightened expectations for the home and their bodies.

In a spinoff article titled 'More Work for Big Mother' (2021), Jathan Sadowski, Yolande Strengers and Jenny Kennedy advance the idea that smart-home technologies are extending new forms of surveillance, automation and data markets into the home under the guise of maternal care (Big Mother).

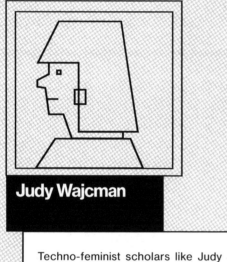

Judy Wajcman

Anne-Jorunn Berg

Techno-feminist scholars like Judy Wajcman have pointed out the absence of women in the design of the (smart) home and argued that traditional feminine concerns have long been ignored by engineering and technology inventions.

In the 1990s, Anne-Jorunn Berg wrote about how women were 'relevant but absent' from smart-home visions, with their knowledge and expertise in housework overlooked in prototypes and neglected as a design resource by male technologists, architects and engineers.

Lynn Spigel

Lynn Spigel analysed early US smart-home visions from 1940–1960, finding that they commonly depicted women liberated from chores in the kitchen, whilst ignoring or undervaluing the labour associated with cleaning, washing and tidying up.

Frances Gabe

Frances Gabe's innovative self-cleaning house was patented in 1984, but has not been pursued in mainstream smart-home designs. Conversely, the contribution of notable home economic and engineering pioneers – like Lillian Gilbreth, Christine Frederick and Ellen Richards – to the design of successful housekeeping devices has been and still is largely overlooked.

Work

HEATHER BERG

What exactly do we mean by work?

Surplus value

How much profit does your labour produce for your employer, and how much are you paid? The difference between the two makes up what Karl Marx's Capital: Vol. IV (first published in 1863) defined as 'surplus value'. Marx calculated this in terms of labour that produced durable goods (e.g. a coat sells for $100; labour, materials and production costs were just $20, so the surplus is $80). This calculation, however, becomes murkier in the context of many of the jobs people who aren't cis men do, such as service work. But employers are still making money off workers' labour, and so surplus value is still being extracted.

→ | ## Work as Exploitation

We spend about one-third of our lives working. But this only accounts for paid jobs. Women (the data assumes a gender binary), who still do the majority of household labour (see: Home p.110.), will spend two-thirds of their lives doing both waged and unwaged work. Let's start with the work we do for wages. Workers in capitalist countries work because we have bills to pay. Think about the phrase 'earning a living'. We have more or less choice about the kinds of jobs we do, but very few people can choose not to work at all. In social democracies, workers have a bit more room to manoeuvre. In these countries, citizens might have some form of support if they take time away from paid work to do caretaking or go to school, or because of a temporary or chronic disability. But most people must go to work even under this kinder version of capitalism. In both cases, employers profit from our work, paying as little as the law and the market will allow.

Gigification, where more and more jobs are precarious and not covered by labour protections, helps employers maximise profit, getting more for less. Because of that other third of their waking hours – the time spent in unpaid household labour – people who aren't cisgender men are more likely to need to do gigged work (see: Trans p.70). Doing gigged work means you are working all the time, but with more flexibility over your day than people who work a nine-to-five job.

The work we do for free – child-rearing, household labour, emotional support, sex – makes someone else money, too (see: Motherhood p.88). But the ways that money flows due to this kind of work are harder to trace. Marxist feminists call this 'reproductive labour' for two reasons: reproduction makes people (i.e. future workers), but it also helps reproduce existing workers by assuring that they are ready to return to their jobs. We reproduce ourselves, too, as when we do self-care to avoid burnout or devote time to education that makes us more effective on the job. Present and future employers profit from unpaid labour. That's why Marxist feminists call all of this 'work'.

But there's a contradiction here that makes reproductive labour potentially powerful even as it's also vulnerable to exploitation: we reproduce ourselves and others as workers, rendering us prone to exploitation, but in the process we also can and do struggle for better futures. Enslaved women, for example, were forced to reproduce children who would bring slave owners profit, but those same families were also important sources of community care and even insurrection.

→ Work as Empowerment

There's another way to think about work. Where anti-capitalist feminists see work through the lens of exploitation, liberal feminists understand paid work through the lens of empowerment. You've likely heard the common story: women were once confined to the home, but as a result of feminism's second wave, they found freedom in paid jobs. (See: Class p.60.) Work became a mode of self-expression and a vehicle for gender equality. Hardworking women could 'lean in', break the glass ceiling and one day could even become bosses too. They could find jobs they loved, and when you love what you do, as the saying goes, 'you'll never work a day in your life'. There is a historical problem with this narrative, however, which is that women of colour, migrants and poor women have always worked (for pay and for free). There's a political problem too: whether you love your job or not, someone's making money off your labour. The best you can hope for if you lean in hard enough is that you become one of the few profiting from the work others do.

→ Gigification

Gigification is the process by which more and more work becomes contingent, short-term and divorced from the benefits and protections associated with stable employment. In order to maximise flexibility and minimise legal responsibilities to workers, employers increasingly shift what were once full-time jobs into short-term or zero-hour contracts. In so doing, they model a growing number of middle-class jobs off the conditions that have long been standard in racialised and feminised jobs, such as farm and domestic labour. Workers under these conditions have few protections if they are injured, harassed or discriminated against at work, and they may spend as much time looking for the next gig as they do getting paid for it.

→ Feminised labour

Feminised labour is labour that looks like the work women have historically done, regardless of the gender identity of whoever does it now. This work is often precarious, demanding emotional as well as physical effort, and has fuzzy boundaries around what's expected and when your day is done. Nursing, food service and teaching are some examples, but more and more jobs in the contemporary economy are becoming 'feminised'. With its boundless hours, lack of worker protections and heavy demands for service with a smile, driving for Uber is a good example of feminised work.

→ Anti-work politics

What if we aimed for an end to work rather than just better conditions whilst doing it or fairer distribution of its profits? That's the promise of anti-work politics, and what Kathi Weeks urges in *The Problem with Work: Feminism, Marxism, and Anti-Work Politics* (Duke University Press, 2011). The political demands that come from this position are different. Trade unions, for example, have historically offered a bargain to employers: give our workers a little bit of security and we'll ensure that they produce more efficiently. Anti-work politics don't take this position. Whilst they support immediate union demands, they might also embrace forms of worker organising that are unproductive and offer no accommodation to bosses. And, following Weeks, they might advocate for a universal basic income (UBI) geared towards freeing us from the compulsion to work in the first place.

Anti-work politics also advocate a shift in our personal politics. If ideas about the work ethic suggest that to be a good worker is to be a good person, anti-work politics reject this. Against the late-capitalist idea that workers must emotionally identify with their jobs – 'love what you do' – anti-work politics push against our identification with work and productivity. What would you do if your days weren't consumed by (paid and unpaid) work?

Suggested Resources

Salt of the Earth (1954)

Chicano zinc miners go on strike for better pay and conditions. At home, their wives face poor conditions and no pay for their reproductive labour. The miners and their wives confront gender inequality alongside racism and labour exploitation. Organising together, they win their strike demands and move towards more equitable relations at home.

Tales of the Night Fairies (2002)

Sex workers in Calcutta organise as the Durbar Mahila Samanwaya Committee. Their community campaigns aim to reduce HIV exposure, keep each other safe from client and police violence, demand the decriminalisation of sex work and form a trade union. The film is also a story about motherhood at the margins, and about poor women's creative survival strategies.

→ Sex Work

'Sex work is work!' proclaim sex worker organisers when they march. But what does it mean to call sex work 'work', and what are the stakes?

Sex workers worldwide insist that sex work is work in order to make a claim for labour rights and against the framing of sex work as either pathological sex or exceptional violence against women. Violence is a feature of sex work, but calling sex work 'work' reminds us of two things:

↓ Violence at Work

■ When sex workers are exposed to violence at work, it's important to mark it as exceptional. Conflating sex work with violence contributes to the idea that sex workers 'sign up' for violence and gives abusers cover.

■ Violence, including sexualised violence, occurs in all forms of work. Likewise, most workers under capitalism consent to work due to limited alternatives. The 'sex work as work' framework rejects the idea that work is free or good at the same time as it advocates for cultural and policy interventions that can make such work safer and better.

H3XTACY / WIKIMEDIA COMMONS

These are feminist concerns because sex work is a feminised profession. Cis and trans women are more likely to do sex work and more likely to be the targets of state surveillance when they do (see: Trans p.70). The risks they encounter from clients, police and others are gendered violence.

↓ Labour Policy

Framing sex work as 'work' changes how we talk about policy. Rather than attempting to criminalise this work out of existence, labour policy seeks to improve working conditions. There are three key approaches to doing this:

1. Decriminalisation, where sex work is governed by local labour law (i.e. regulations concerning minimum wages and maximum hours worked, protections for those who unionise, policies governing freedom of contract and consent to work) and existing law regarding sexual consent. In this model, workers are not subject to sex work–specific licensing or zoning requirements. Most workers prefer this model and say that it makes them better able to organise collectively, seek help when clients are abusive and advertise and screen clients without fear of police surveillance.

2. Legalisation, where workers are subject to sex work–specific licensing and/or zoning requirements. Workers must register with the state under their legal names. Most workers say that this model restricts their autonomy, though it is preferable to criminalisation. In the legalised brothels in Nevada (USA), for example, workers must register with the state, they (but not their clients) are tested for sexually transmitted infections, and business licensing requirements favour capitalised brothel owners rather than sex workers working independently.

3. Partial criminalisation (or 'the Nordic Model') decriminalises the sale but not the purchase of sex. Here, sex workers continue to face the risks associated with labouring in an underground market. What's more, most do not want their clients criminalised because they need to continue to make a living.

Organisation Spotlights

Sex Workers Education & Advocacy Taskforce (SWEAT), Cape Town, South Africa

Associação das Prostitutas de Minas Gerais (APROSMIG), Rio de Janeiro, Brazil

Gays and Lesbians Living in a Transgender Society (GLITS), New York, USA

Centre for Sex Workers' Protection (EMPOWER), Patpong, Thailand

→ | Organising and Workplace Struggle

There is a long history of gender non-conforming and women-led resistance to capitalist workplace injustice.

Women and gender-non-conforming people have long pursued better pay and working conditions through traditional trade unions. Finding power in collectivity, they've won higher wages, safer conditions, shorter hours (and the weekend!), protection from sexual harassment and a host of other concessions from their employers. Threatening strikes, they remind employers that 'labour creates all wealth' (as the unionist Eugene Debs put it) and that when the work stops, wealth generation does too. During the Progressive Era, for example, women garment workers in industrialised countries struck until their demands for better wages, safer workplaces and an end to child labour were met. Today, the organising of garment workers in the Global South centres on similar demands.

Two major workplace disasters a century apart show the historical continuity: in 1911 in New York City, 146 garment workers (mostly women, girls and migrants) died in what would become known as the Triangle Shirtwaist Factory fire. Their employer had locked all exits in an effort to prevent workers from taking breaks. In 2013 in Bangladesh, 1,100 workers (again mostly women) died when their factory collapsed. Owners had ignored warnings that the building was structurally unsound. Feminist labour scholars remind us that whilst these incidents were disastrous, they were not accidents: workplace injury and death are par for the course in an economy that prioritises profit over worker well-being and in regulatory environments that primarily serve employers. Racialised women will continue to be disproportionally vulnerable under this system.

Even as they've pursued trade union politics, women and gender-non-conforming people have confronted misogyny from trade unions' traditional leadership of cis men. Today, however, trade unions' most vibrant sectors are often among the feminised workers who would have once been excluded. Hotel and home healthcare workers are some examples.

Another set of organising tactics are less formal but no less impactful. Underground tactics such as workplace sabotage, slowdowns, feigned incompetence and workplace theft might be particularly attractive to feminised workers who find that their concerns are outside the purview of traditional trade unionising. Domestic workers, for example, have historically laboured under conditions of isolation and invisibility. But they might use those to their advantage by stealing from abusive employers. Restaurant workers might purposefully fail a health inspection, or flight attendants might all decide to call in sick on the same day. Workers may pursue these tactics on an individual basis (e.g. one factory worker causes a machine to break in order to get more break time) or collectively (e.g. social workers decide together to ignore a racist and classist policy requiring them to turn mums in to child protective services for co-sleeping arrangements, but never formally notify their employer of the policy change). Workers' massive withdrawal from low-waged work in the COVID-pandemic era is an example of another informal tactic: work refusal.

Health and Medicine

CELIA ROBERTS

Struggles over bodies and health have always been central to feminism.

→ ## Contesting medicine: the rise of women's health movements

Feminist engagements with health are deeply entwined with activism and struggle. Changes to health care and to health itself are one of the great success stories of feminist politics across the globe. Practices that many of us now take for granted – doctors sharing information with patients and patients being invited to make collaborative decisions with clinicians, for example – are the result of feminist activism.

In Britain, feminist activism around health started in the late nineteenth century; campaigns around syphilis were one of the founding elements of so-called first-wave feminism (see: Class p.60 and textbox opposite on Nineteenth-Century British Feminists and Syphilis). Through the twentieth century, women's health campaigns appeared around the world, and from the 1980s onwards, forming – particularly the US – into what is now described as 'the Women's Health Movement.' The use of 'the' in this phrase is problematic: feminist health activism is actually highly dispersed and fluid. Women's health movements are a global phenomenon, with all the positives and negatives associated with this. Whilst the spread of knowledge about female bodies is incredibly important, sometimes health activists have imported particular medical and health-related knowledge and practices to other places without adequately considering where they came from and what they assume.

Feminist activists have also shaped knowledge of health and bodies through putting their own bodies at the heart of their investigations and listening carefully and systematically to the voices and experiences of women. In the late 1960s and early 1970s, the Boston Women's Health Collective, for example, started with gathering in people's homes to discuss bodies, medicine and health. Members developed practises or protocols of collective self-examination, particularly of genitals and reproductive systems. Knowledge gathered through these practices was collated and published in the now-famous book *Our Bodies, Ourselves*, which has been translated into thirty-three languages and published in nine US editions, inspiring many spinoffs. The key aims of this movement were to produce and evaluate knowledge about health from women's experience and to contest sexist accounts of women's differences from men.

The question of bio-psycho-social differences between groups of people is at the heart of feminist research and activism around health and medicine (see textbox on Bio-Psycho-Social). Medicine has to make assumptions about similarities and understand differences well. Doctors have to know what a health variation or difference is and what indicates a disease or potential health problem. For example, in what ways does a diseased heart look different to a healthy one? To come to understand this key difference, medical science observes and compares many cases in order to learn what healthy variation is and when clinicians should be concerned. Variations in bodies are caused by many factors: genetic differences, physical experiences such as exposure to viruses and psychosocial experiences such as economic or emotional deprivation, racism or sexism. Feminist activists and researchers have successfully fought to have the complexities of differences recognised, and to expose the multiple ways in which conventional medical science (historically produced by privileged men) has made unjust assumptions about what constituted health.

Nineteenth-Century British Feminists and Syphilis

So-called first-wave feminism was deeply concerned with sexuality and health. In 1864, British police were given the power to register women sex workers, to subject them to medical testing for syphilis and to detain those found to have this condition. Feminists led by Josephine Butler argued that it was both discriminatory and irrational to detain these women without attempting to medically test or change the behaviour of the men who were using their services. Their campaigns led to the repeal of the Contagious Diseases Act (1864), which gave police these powers, in 1886.

Bio-Psycho-Social

This unwieldy term refers to the interwoven and often inextricably connected biological, social and psychological forces that shape our bodies and health. Thinking of breast cancer, for example, we might consider an individual's family history of cancer (genetic and otherwise), their personal exposure to environmental toxins and medicines and their experiences of diet, exercise, smoking and stress as twisting together to produce their risk of developing illness.

→ Paying Attention to Sex/Gender Differences

Feminists have successfully contested biomedical research and the way it frames health and illness.

In many strands of medical research, although importantly not in every case, marginalised men (sometimes those in prisons or asylums) have historically been used as research subjects, as if they could somehow stand in for all humans. Women of reproductive age were excluded from many pharmaceutical trials, for example, because of potential risk to fetuses if they became pregnant during the research. Potentially important differences of race/ethnicity, dis/ability, geographic location and social class have also often been overlooked in the conclusions drawn from medical research.

Feminists have argued that such practices have left substantial gaps in medical knowledge about women's bodies and the effects of medications and other interventions on them. Heart disease is a key example here. Heart disease affects men and has long been studied as a male problem. This has had significant impact on public health campaigns and citizens' knowledge about heart health. Because it has been considered as a male problem, women are less likely to recognise the signs of heart disease and thus more likely to miss out on important early interventions. Autism has had a similar history. Seen as a 'problem' more commonly experienced by men and boys (indeed, autism has been controversially described as 'excessive maleness'), women and girls have been less likely to receive a timely diagnosis or to be offered early interventions. Feminists' calls to pay attention to the ways in which assumptions about bodies structure medical knowledge have been important in challenging knowledge and practices in many areas of health and medicine. It is increasingly inconceivable for researchers and clinicians to use male bodies as the norm or to ignore other important differences such as race/ethnicity and social class.

Feminists have had to fight hard to get conventional medicine to pay serious attention to female bodies and to diseases or conditions that women and girls are more likely to experience. Breast cancer is an interesting example. Although it is hard to imagine now, in the 1970s breast cancer was a little-researched and poorly understood condition shrouded in shame. In the 1980s, feminist activists challenged conventional medical approaches to treating breast cancer, which were highly invasive and had poor outcomes. Over more than two decades, breast cancer activists changed medical understandings and interventions around breast cancer, including screening, lumpectomies, mastectomies and prevention. Unfortunately, since the turn of the twenty-first century, elements of breast cancer activism, including the pink ribbon itself, have been captured by corporations looking to increase sales. This is described by contemporary feminist activists as pink washing.

Mental health is another arena in which feminists have had a substantial impact in both de-stigmatising and in producing new understandings of the causes and best treatments for many conditions. Early feminist research on depression, for example, argued that women's mental health difficulties often had strong connections to experiences of sexual abuse, domestic violence and forms of social oppression. Contesting conventional psychiatric accounts of mental illness as neurological disease or neurochemical imbalance, feminist activists and scholars (many of whom were also survivors of psychiatric treatment) argued that mental illness should be understood as communicating profound dissatisfactions or fears that are actually meaningful reactions to unbearable life situations.

→ Normal Birth

Pregnancy and birth are important arenas for feminist politics. Struggles are fierce and ongoing in many places.

Experiences of pregnancy and birth vary widely across the world. Whilst some people have access to the latest developments in medical and digital technologies – which track and test ovulation and pregnancy, medically assist conception, medically assess fetuses and maximise the chances of safe birth and a healthy start to a baby's life – millions of women conceive, gestate and give birth to children without any medical assistance or intervention whatsoever. These women and children are more likely to encounter serious health challenges, including untreated infertility, genetic disease, miscarriage and damage or even death during or immediately after birth. In addition, many women still have little or no access to birth control or abortion and give birth to children they are unable or unwilling to parent.

In wealthier parts of the world, pregnancy and birth remain firmly within the domain of medicine. As 1970s feminists argued, in earlier centuries, knowledgeable women were responsible for pre- and post-natal care and assisting at births. During the development of modern science from the 1750s, male scientists and clinicians gradually wrested this control from women, ignoring or appropriating centuries of accumulated knowledge. In many Euro-American countries, birth became highly managed. Women gave birth in hospitals and were subjected to traumatising practices such as shaving, enemas, episiotomies, the widespread use of forceps and anaesthetising medications and medically unnecessary Caesarean sections. In the 1960s and '70s, feminist activists joined forces with other women concerned about birth trauma to campaign for natural or 'normal' birth. Emphasising women's right to choose where, when and how to give birth, they argued that birth should be reclaimed as a positive, healthy experience. Women should, they claimed, be taught about birth and supported so that they could give birth safely. Importantly, this was not an argument against medical intervention when

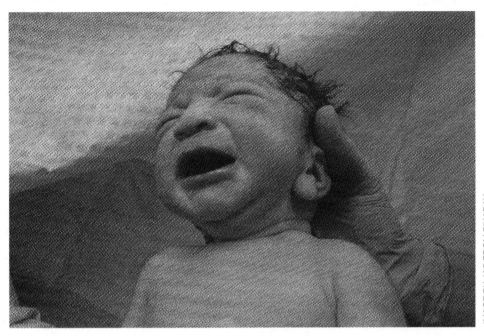

things go wrong, but a move away from an assumption that medical control was always better, or, indeed, positive for infant and maternal health.

Ongoing feminist struggles to improve pregnancy and birth emphasise the importance of women's knowledge and experience, and in this way have connections to earlier practices of midwifery. Midwife-led birthing clinics and doula services are available in many parts of the Global North today. Many more women are now working as doctors and in medical research, which is also part of the wider reshaping of medicine's relation to women's bodies and reproduction more broadly.

In many ways, however, medical and scientific knowledge retain a strong grip on conception, pregnancy and birth. The rise of digital fertility monitoring, the corporatisation of reproductive medicine and increased pressures on young women to think of themselves as potentially infertile (and to act prudently by freezing their eggs) demonstrate that reproduction is a sphere of profit making in our times. Although the safety of pregnancy and birth have improved for many people, and feminist campaigns have made important changes in this space, reproduction remains entangled in politics and heavily regulated.

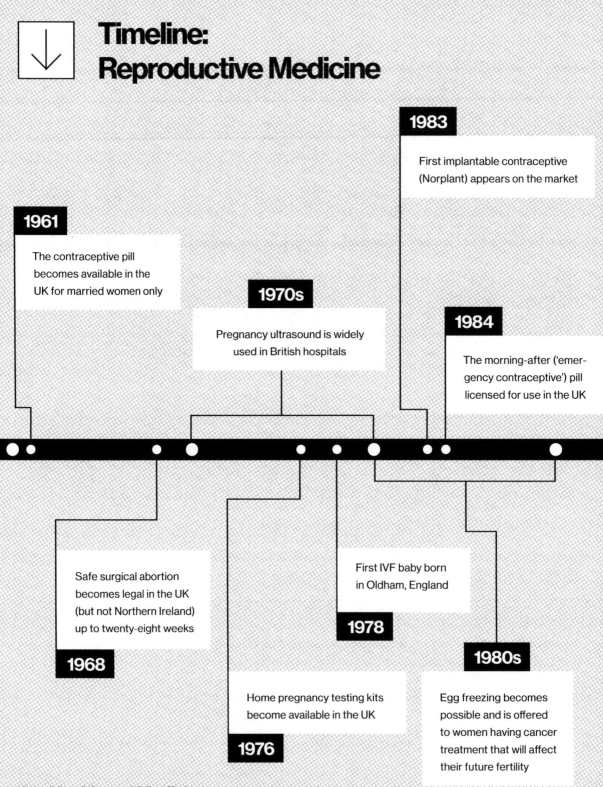

Timeline: Reproductive Medicine

1983
First implantable contraceptive (Norplant) appears on the market

1961
The contraceptive pill becomes available in the UK for married women only

1970s
Pregnancy ultrasound is widely used in British hospitals

1984
The morning-after ('emergency contraceptive') pill licensed for use in the UK

Safe surgical abortion becomes legal in the UK (but not Northern Ireland) up to twenty-eight weeks
1968

First IVF baby born in Oldham, England
1978

1980s
Egg freezing becomes possible and is offered to women having cancer treatment that will affect their future fertility

Home pregnancy testing kits become available in the UK
1976

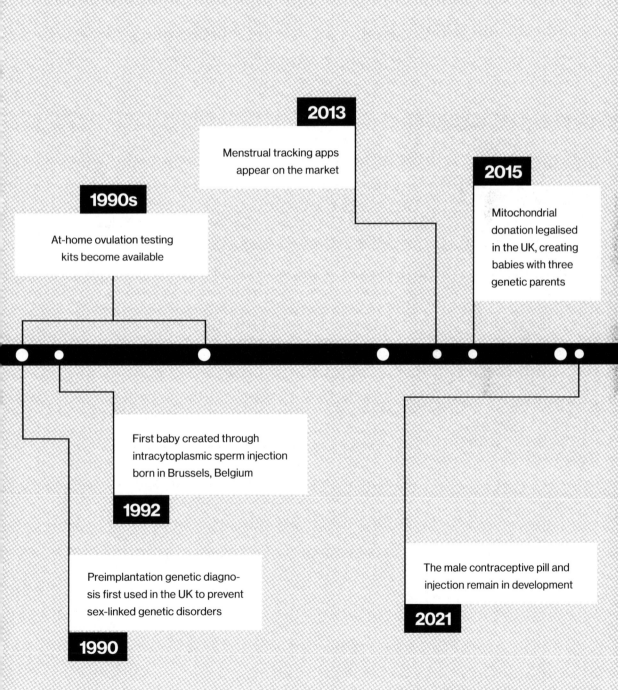

2013

Menstrual tracking apps appear on the market

2015

Mitochondrial donation legalised in the UK, creating babies with three genetic parents

1990s

At-home ovulation testing kits become available

First baby created through intracytoplasmic sperm injection born in Brussels, Belgium

1992

Preimplantation genetic diagnosis first used in the UK to prevent sex-linked genetic disorders

1990

The male contraceptive pill and injection remain in development

2021

Technology

YOLANDE STRENGERS

The gendering of technology has changed substantially over time.

Smothered by Invention: Technology in Women's Lives, edited by Wendy Faulkner and Erik Arnold (Pluto Press, 1985), is a cornerstone text which argues that technology is a means by which men exercise control over women in the context of housework, paid work and reproductive medicine. Contributors to this provocative collection maintain that technology is allied to masculinity and excludes women. Women do not control technology but become objects of technological control and intervention, particularly with respect to the efficiency and productivity of their economic, domestic and reproductive labour.

→ ## Is Technology Gendered?

The short answer is yes, but not inherently. Some technologies are gendered by design, whereas others have historically been associated with certain genders that relate to expected social roles. In some cases, technology amplifies these gendered distinctions (see textbox on White and Black Goods). We might think of a gendered division between high-tech goods or gadgets ('toys for the boys') and low-tech ones, or between the masculine heavy machinery of the pre-information age factory and feminine domestic technologies like cookers and washing machines. This can become a chicken-and-egg scenario, where historical stereotypes about who wants and uses certain technologies are exaggerated through design and marketing, thereby reinforcing binary gendered associations. The assumption designers and marketeers make about who is more likely to use a given technology has often led to its association with a given gender, although non-binary technologies have always existed and will hopefully become more prevalent. Technology is also gendered through the values it prioritises in our workplaces, homes and lives. For instance, Taylorist principles of efficiency and productivity have become imbued in workplace and industrial technologies, as well as in so-called labour-saving devices designed for the home.

→ Has Technology Become Less Gendered over Time?

Whilst some gendered associations with technology have weakened over time, others have become further entrenched. For instance, advanced and 'frontier' technologies, particularly in the fields of the military, security and space, are highly masculinised. These professional fields are also dominated by men, which shapes the types of solutions and technologies that are designed and prioritised.

Artificial Intelligence (AI) has become increasingly gendered by design, through the introduction of anthropomorphised and feminised voices and personas (see: Feminine by Design p.152). This male-dominated field has also been criticised for perpetuating gender and racial biases that have been found to diminish, erase or negatively represent the experiences of women and minority, vulnerable or disadvantaged groups (see: Bias at the Frontiers p.148).

Taylorism

In *Principles of Scientific Management* (1911), Frederick Winslow Taylor devised a theory of management that would improve efficiency and productivity in the manufacturing industry. The concept of Taylorism refers to the persistence of his ideas in all aspects of our lives: an obsession with time, optimisation (including self-optimisation) and increased standardisation.

White and Black Goods

'White goods' (cookers, washing machines and refrigerators) have typically been marketed towards women, whereas marketing for 'black goods' (televisions, stereo systems and other audiovisual technologies) has targeted men. These stereotypes, while perhaps not as stark as during the twentieth century, still linger today and are appearing in new forms.

Where Are the Women?

Throughout the nineteenth century and up to World War II, computer programming was largely considered women's work and was a field pioneered by women like Ada Lovelace and Grace Hopper. However, as the 'soft work' associated with computation evolved into modern software, and as personal computers started making their way into homes and (boys') bedrooms, women's representation in the sector began to decline. Nowadays, women are vastly underrepresented in many technical disciplines and professions, particularly at the frontiers of technology development, such as in the fields of AI, cybersecurity and software engineering.

There are many reasons for this. They extend from how we socialise girls and boys from a young age to cultivate an interest (or not) in computing through to the unbalanced and unwelcoming environments that are reported by women who work and study in technology fields and companies. One of the key problems has been the prevalence of stereotypically masculine 'geek' associations with technologies, which have led to girls stepping away from computing interests and disciplines. More recently, over-confident and charismatic masculine leaders originating from Silicon Valley's Big Tech companies have reinforced stereotypes of tech success as predominantly white and male. This 'Brotopia', as journalist Emily Chang describes it, has led to a 'boys' club' culture that discourages women from participating and succeeding in computing fields.

Suggested Resources

Chang, Emily. *Brotopia: Breaking Up the Boys' Club of Silicon Valley*. Penguin Random House, 2019.

Margolis, Jane, and Allan Fisher. *Unlocking the Clubhouse: Women in Computing*. MIT Press, 2001.

Hicks, Mar. *Programmed Inequality: How Britain Discarded Women Technologists and Lost Its Edge in Computing*. MIT Press, 2017.

Will Tech Save the World?

Technology solutionist narratives are overly optimistic and often ignore more socially just alternatives.

There is a growing focus on techno-fixes and technology solutions to address a raft of social and environmental problems. Increasingly, Big Tech companies, led mostly by white able-bodied men, are positioning themselves as the saviours of earth and humanity by offering 'solutions' to problems like the care crisis around an ageing population (e.g. assistive care robots), housework (e.g. smart-home devices) or climate change (e.g. electric vehicles and big batteries). Some of these entrepreneurs are also searching for a 'Planet B' (e.g. through the space race between billionaires Elon Musk of Tesla and Jeff Bezos of Amazon). These solutions are often proposed in the absence of public policy, or as part of public-private partnerships which shift responsibility for many contemporary challenges away from governments and publics and onto corporate or private enterprises.

NICKYPE VIA PIXABAY

Surveillance Capitalism

Shoshana Zuboff's landmark book, *Surveillance Capitalism*, has been instrumental in high-lighting the growing issues associated with Big Tech companies' increasing use of data surveillance to expand their markets and influence. Zuboff describes surveil-lance capitalism as 'parasitic and self-referential' (like a vampire); it feeds off human emotions and experience, and packages this data as commodities for third parties to target products, content and services towards people. The aim, Zuboff contends, is to 'automate us' towards the capitalist ends of Big Tech by enrolling us in new data and technology markets. The tech-niques used are often extrac-tive, unethical and manipulative, and leave marginalised groups more vulnerable to these tech-niques and markets.

Technofeminist and ecofeminist scholars have critiqued these approaches for failing to provide ethical and sustainable futures that, for instance, revalue how we remunerate care work in the social care sector, or pursue and promote lifestyles that don't depend on increasing consumption and waste. Many commen-tators are also troubled by the increasing power held by Big Tech companies, which are motivated by their profits, market control and influence through surveillance capitalism, not by social or environmental justice issues. Likewise, the utopian narratives that dominate many contemporary debates mask the uneven labour and environmental effects of mining, production and e-waste associated with the technological solutions proposed. In this regard, most Big Tech 'saviours' have dubious and concerning track records with regards to their environmental impacts (e.g. from mineral extraction to e-waste) and working conditions.

Timeline: Hovercraft, Robot Vacuums and Sexbots

1952–1968

Astro Boy (Mighty Atom)

The Japanese manga and anime series Astro Boy stars a young android with human emotions, and is cited by many Japanese roboticists as the inspiration for their designs.

1950   **1960**   **1970**   **1980**

1962–1963

Rosie-the-robot from *The Jetsons*

Housekeeping robot Rosie from the American animated sitcom *The Jetsons* has set the aspirational standard for many smart-home devices, and is cited as the inspiration for some designs, including the Roomba robotic vacuum cleaner. However, some argue Rosie has set an unattainable goal for the smart-home industry that continually leaves consumers disappointed.

1966–

Star Trek's computer assistant

Star Trek's conversational computer was the inspiration for Amazon's Alexa voice assistant and other digital voice assistants. American actress Majel Barrett-Roddenberry was the female voice behind the computer throughout the series, from 1966 to 2009.

Who imagines emerging technologies? And where do new ideas come from? Science fiction (another male-dominated field) has provided inspiration for many of the emerging technologies we live with or fear today, as well as the blueprints for ones that many still desire to manifest in real life. Here are some examples that have inspired companies, designers and technologists during the twentieth and twenty-first centuries.

2001–

Cortana from Microsoft's *Halo* video game franchise

Cortana is a fictional and sexualised AI character in the *Halo* video game series who provides tactical information for the player, who often assumes the role of Master Chief. The character inspired Microsoft's virtual assistant of the same name.

1985–1990

The *Back to the Future* films provided the blueprint for many aspirational technology designs, such as flying cars, hovercrafts, wearable tech, augmented-reality glasses and intelligent home appliances. They continue to inspire the design of emerging technologies today.

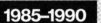

1990

2000

2010

1984–

The Terminator android

The Terminator films and their depiction of relentless killing machines have exacerbated long-standing concerns and fears in the West about AI and robots taking over. To counteract these fears, technology companies have prioritised designs that appear cute, friendly and harmless.

2017

Blade Runner gynoids and holograms

Blade Runner 2049 and *Blade Runner* (1982) draw on tropes and stereotypes of women in service or sexual roles in the characterisation of their feminised AI characters. These imaginaries have been linked to the design of feminised AI like digital voice assistants and sex robots.

→ Bias at the Frontiers

Bias continues to plague technology development, particularly AI.

Whilst bias – an inclination or prejudice for or against a particular person or group – has always been an issue with technology, it is now a well-known problem in the design and operation of emerging technologies involving machine-learning, algorithms, conversation design and robotics. The most advanced fields of technology, which are also the most male-dominated, are where biases are most commonly amplified in ways that disadvantage or disrespect certain groups of people – particularly anyone who is not white, cisgender, male or able-bodied. Once identified or exposed, those responsible for reproducing biases through technology often attempt to fix the problem; however, new biases emerge all the time, and significant damage can occur to individuals and/or groups before biases are detected and resolved.

↓ How Can We Understand Bias?

There are many different ways to understand bias. For instance, we can think of bias as unconscious, where implicit stereotypes or assumptions implicitly shape how we view certain people or situations; conscious, where explicit stereotypes and assumptions about certain groups of people are expressed through harassment or exclusionary tactics; and algorithmic, where systematic and repeatable programming decisions or data training protocols privilege one group over another to create inequitable outcomes (either by human design or accident). These biases overlap; for instance, algorithmic bias can be an outcome of both unconscious and conscious biases.

Biases affect technology design, marketing and use, and have broader impacts in society. For instance, technology can amplify existing biases when they are trained on corpuses of material (images or texts) that already contain gendered or racial stereotypes, assumptions or biases. For instance, Google's search engines were exposed by Safiya Umoja Noble as being racially and sexually biased. A Google search for 'Black girls' would bring up sexually explicit references and imagery, whereas a search for 'professional women' would bring up images of white women with straight hair.

Technologies can be biased through users' interactions with them, which 'teach' machine-learning systems how to behave. Microsoft's Twitter bot Tay is an example of this. The chat-bot 'learned' (through interaction with Twitter users) to spout anti-Semitism, racism, Nazism and sexism within twelve hours of being released.

Industries with a lack of diversity in their workforce, like technology sectors and advanced computing fields, have been strongly linked to the reproduction of biases. Likewise, a failure to test new technology designs with diverse users can lead to biases towards one user group. For instance, UNESCO has linked the male dominance in technology fields to the design of feminised digital voice assistants, which reinforce gender biases and stereotypes about women in assistive and submissive roles (see: Feminine by Design p.152). Likewise, smartphones have been criticised for being too big for many women's hands, and self-tracking health apps have been criticised for not tracking menstruation and other women's health issues.

The AI Now Institute has made a number of recommendations to address bias and discrimination in the industry. These include diversifying the workforce, being transparent in the tracking and publicising of AI systems, engaging in rigorous testing with diverse users, conducting wider social analysis on how AI is used in context and questioning whether certain systems should be designed at all, given the high likelihood (according to risk assessments) of their potential to reproduce biases.

↓ Types of Bias

Algorithmic bias

- Detecting sexuality from headshots, which can only identify gender binaries (male/female) and can miscategorise people with non-stereotypical attributes.

- Determining 'beauty' and emotions from facial datasets (that are more likely to categorise people of colour as ugly and angry).

- Assessing employability through CVs that prioritise one gender or race over others.

- Predicting 'criminality' based on facial features or racial characteristics, which are more likely to categorise Black people as potential (re)offenders.

Unconscious bias

- Hiring people that look like you or fit the stereotype of success.

- Training voice algorithms according to a dominant set of users so that they struggle to understand other voices (e.g. women and people with diverse accents).

- Failing to consider or include the experiences or insights from a particular group of people (e.g. older adults).

Conscious bias

- Actively discriminating against people based on gender, race or other attributes.

- Harassing people based on gender, race or other attributes.

- Allowing a particular view or position to inform the programming or design of AI (or deliberately excluding a particular view or position).

- Designing sex robots for male sexual pleasure.

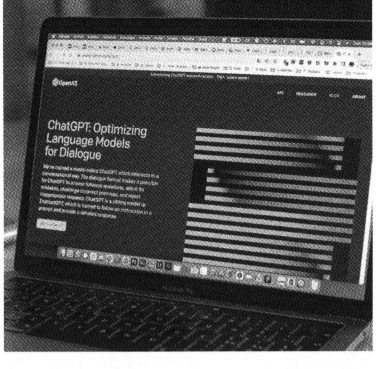

EMILIANO VITTORIOSI / UNSPLASH

Suggested Resources

Eubanks, Virginia. *Automating Inequality: How High-Tech Tools Profile, Police, and Punish the Poor*. St Martin's Press, 2019.

Noble, Safiya Umoja. *Algorithms of Oppression: How Search Engines Reinforce Racism*. New York University Press, 2018.

Wachter-Boettcher, Sarah. *Technically Wrong: Sexist Apps, Biased Algorithms, and Other Threats of Toxic Tech*. W. W. Norton, 2018.

Myers West, Sarah, Meredith Whittaker and Kate Crawford. *Discriminating Systems: Gender, Race, and Power in AI*. AI Now Institute, 2019, https://ainowinstitute.org/discriminatingsystems.pdf.

↓ Chat GPT

Advanced AI chatbots, like OpenAI's ChatGPT (publicly launched in 2022) have attracted significant attention for their articulate and detailed answers to a broad range of questions and topics. ChatGPT's functionality is versatile and comprehensive: it can compose poems and songs, write and debug computer programs, answer complex questions, and write job applications, articles or essays. While ChatGPT has been trained to minimise harmful or deceitful responses, it is not free from bias. The chatbot has been accused of political bias (most commonly anti-conservative or left leaning bias). However, a bigger concern for feminists is how the language models of chatbots like ChatGPT gain access to data and knowledge. In 2020, OpenAI claimed that their language model, which has 175 billion parameters, was the largest ever created. Many of these inputs reflect the biases of their original human authors, and the underrepresentation of women's and children's voices and people who speak languages other than English (or nonstandard English). Chatbots like ChatGPT, which synthesise large quantities of data to generate predictive text, amplify the marginalisation of certain biases and voices rather than correcting the imbalance.

→ Feminine by Design

Feminine assistants and robots hark back to problematic nostalgic stereotypes about women and housewives.

There is a trend to feminise conversational and anthropomorphised robots and devices, such as voice assistants, assistive and care robots and sex robots. This can take place through giving these technologies female voices and names, feminised forms or bodies and feminised roles and tasks. Feminist scholars have argued that these technologies are increasingly implicated in various roles and labours that are reminiscent of the ideal 1950s housewife (see: Home p.110). This can be viewed as a deliberate design decision – or conscious bias – where technology companies use stereotypes of friendly, helpful and caring (white) feminine personas to endear users towards these technologies. Typically, these devices and robots provide a service, and are therefore imbued with subservient and service-oriented characteristics that position them as non-threatening and comforting, making users less concerned about the devices' potential negative effects, such as how they can enrol people in surveillance capitalist markets.

Common critiques of this feminisation are that it reinforces common biases about women in society (such as being docile, friendly, helpful) and potentially undermines progress towards gender equality. For example, digital voice assistant personalities reinforce the idea that administrative, service and caring tasks are women's responsibility. Scholars have shown how the feminisation of technology can lead to (and sometimes condone) sexualised and gendered abuse being directed towards them.

Likewise, the de-racialisation of voice assistants and their aesthetic coding as educated, native-speaking, white women has been critiqued by critical race scholars for mimicking a servant/master relationship between the device and users.

ED EMSHWILLER, PUBLIC DOMAIN, VIA WIKIMEDIA COMMONS

Suggested Resources

Bergen, Hilary. '"I'd Blush if I Could": Digital Assistants, Disembodied Cyborgs and the Problem of Gender'. *Word and Text: A Journal of Literary Studies and Linguistics 1* (2016): 95–113.

Phan, Thao. 'Amazon Echo and the Aesthetics of Whiteness'. *Catalyst* 5, no. 1 (2019).

Strengers, Yolande, and Jenny Kennedy. *The Smart Wife*. MIT Press, 2020.

Sweeney, Miriam. 'Not Just a Pretty (Inter)face: A Critical Analysis of Microsoft's "Ms. Dewey"'. PhD diss., University of Illinois, 2013.

West, Mark, Rebecca Kraut and Chew Han Ei. *I'd Blush if I Could: Closing Gender Divides in Digital Skills through Education*. UNESCO and EQUALS Skills Coalition, 2019, https://en.unesco.org/Id-blush-if-I-could.

↓ | Bitches with Glitches

The feminisation of digital voice assistants and assistive robots has led to their characterisation as 'bitches with glitches' by Yolande Strengers and Jenny Kennedy. This refers to the way in which malfunctions and negative experiences with these devices are blamed on their feminised moods, personalities or innate biological inferiority. These characterisations occur in large public or private forums (e.g. at consumer shows and events), in the media, on user forums and in individuals' accounts of their experiences. For instance, media articles reporting malfunctions with devices often blame the feminised AI, rather than the male-dominated tech companies that designed and programmed the device. Similarly, terminology such as 'hysterical', 'manic', 'terrifying', 'bitch mode' or giving users the 'silent treatment' is used to describe these malfunctions. These negative associations reinforce negative stereotypes about women in society.

Our hope is that this book will serve as a resource and a road map that will inspire each and every reader to continue exploring, thinking about, discussing and 'doing' feminism.

It is not an end but a beginning.

AND IT IS FOR EVERYBODY.